WHERE
WILTSHIRE
MEETS
SOMERSET

Cover: Iford House and bridge

Corsley Church and Cley Hill

WHERE WILTSHIRE MEETS SOMERSET

20 Walks in the Country around Bath, Bradford-on-Avon, Trowbridge, Westbury, Warminster and Frome

Roger Jones

With Illustrations by Edward Dowden

Ex Libris Press

First published 1982
Revised edition 1985

Ex Libris Press
1 The Shambles
Bradford-on-Avon
Wiltshire

Typeset by Quadraset Ltd, Midsomer Norton, Bath, Avon

Printed in Great Britain by Midway Press, Gay Street, Bath, Avon

ISBN 0 95065 633 X

Other books by Roger Jones:

A Book of Newton Abbot
Rambles around Newton Abbot
Wiltshire Rambles
Down the Bristol Avon
The Walker's Companion

Roger Jones lives in Bradford-on-Avon where he and his wife run the Ex Libris Bookshop. They have three children and moved to Wiltshire from South Devon in 1980. Although a Londoner by birth, the author has grown to love the countryside not only for its natural beauty but also for its endless fascination, and he firmly believes that walking is the best way to truly appreciate both.

Edward Dowden is a professional artist who moved to Bradford-on-Avon from Northumberland in 1980. His primary interests are landscape and architecture, and he works in all mediums. Examples of his work, both originals and prints, may be viewed at the Linfield Galleries in Bradford-on-Avon.

CONTENTS

INTRODUCTION

When I came to live in Bradford-on-Avon in the summer of 1980 I set about exploring the countryside around the town at my first opportunity. I had lived in South Devon for four years at a spot within easy reach of both the Coast Path and Dartmoor National Park, so I was rather spoilt for beauty and variety in my walking.

My first walks out of Bradford were along the towpath of the Kennet and Avon Canal towards Avoncliff, where I found a country as attractive as much in South Devon. Here the River Avon flows through a steep-sided valley which is garlanded by woods and studded with villages built from the stone of the hills on which they stand. The prospect of Bradford from Barton Farm is very striking, particularly in the morning when the risen sun casts its light directly onto the terraces stacked one above the other on the south-east facing slope. The natural stone shines brilliantly, almost magically, as though it were somehow lit from within.

Turleigh is set high in a cleft on the north bank of the Avon and is followed by Avoncliff which is set lower in the valley close by the mills which were once active on both banks. Farther down river come Freshford and Limpley Stoke. These are all pleasant villages yet I remain especially attracted to the point where the Rivers Frome and Avon unite, where the Frome valley from the south widens to meet the Avon from the east. The stone bridge by 'The Inn' at Freshford, the verdant meadows on the floodplain of the two rivers, the wooded eminence of Staples Hill: all combine to present a vision of great charm and tranquillity. At my first visit there I found the prospect up the Frome valley a great lure. Soon afterwards, as I pressed on along the canal towards Dundas aqueduct, the valley of the Midford Brook looked equally enticing.

We had moved into a house in the north-east corner of Bradford-on-Avon. As Woolley Street rises towards Woolley Green, the houses are replaced by fields which slope away to the south east, across a wide vale in which Trowbridge is situated, and on towards the chalk escarpment of Salisbury Plain. The White Horse is visible from here, unless obscured by the plume of smoke from the cement works just below. Depending on the weather and the position of the sun, the chalk escarpment can appear very dramatic: like a great tidal wave suddenly frozen in its path westwards, and always as a most prominent feature in the landscape.

The hillside upon which much of old Bradford stands is composed of the creamy yellow limestone of which the Cotswold Hills and its towns and villages are made. A cursory examination of a geological map of the area assured me that, geologically speaking at least, Bradford-on-Avon stands on the slope of a hill that forms the south-eastern edge of the Cotswold range. It is interesting to note that the topographical writer, H. J. Massingham, in his book *Cotswold Country*,* deals with the limestone belt which touches ten counties between Dorset and Lincolnshire. Massingham recognised the diversity yet underlying unity of that limestone belt, or 'Cotswold Country', in terms of geology, landscape and building materials.

The western scarp of Salisbury Plain was another feature beckoning me, and so naturally were the towns which lie at its feet, namely Trowbridge, Westbury and Warminster. The Somerset–Wiltshire border runs more or less north–south a few miles to the west of this string of towns, and even nearer to Bradford-on-Avon. I followed the valleys of the River Frome and the Midford Brook as they cross the county boundary into Somerset and I am quite convinced that the countryside changes in doing so. On the Somerset side the country seems more broken, more closely divided into hill and vale, somehow more intimate and more like the South Devon with which I was familiar. The Wiltshire side seems characterised more by open spaces, whether upland or lowland.

Cley Hill is an outpost of the Wiltshire chalk just north of the Longleat estate from which one can see Warminster to the east and Frome in Somerset to the west, or north west and, beyond it, the Mendips. It seemed natural that I should extend my wanderings to Frome and its surroundings. After an initial visit to the town I was hooked. It has a charm and an attraction totally different to that of Bradford or the other towns along the Somerset–Wiltshire border. It is unique among them in being a market town complete with weekly livestock market. It was as important a centre of the wool and clothing trades as Bradford and Trowbridge, and has the fascinating Trinity estate of artisans' houses built in the seventeenth and eighteenth centuries. This industrial housing is far removed from the drab rows of identical dwellings which were the norm during the industrial revolution of a later century.

It was during this time that the clothing industry, which was the staple of Frome's prosperity, was lost to the new centres of production in the north of England. This meant that, like Bradford, Frome was never much affected by Victorian expansion and redevelopment and both towns maintain the appearance and atmosphere of an earlier era. Frome lacks the architectural riches of Bradford but has instead all manner of interesting backwaters, as befits an old market town.

In the triangle between Frome, Bath and Bradford-on-Avon there lies a relatively sparsely populated hinterland which is largely dependent on agriculture but which harbours such interesting and attractive villages as Lullington, Wellow and Norton St Philip, all of which are well worth exploring.

In the area dealt with in this book, we find a diversity of landscape

*H. J. MASSINGHAM, *Cotswold Country*, Batsford, 1937.

represented by the borders of the Mendips, the Cotswolds and Salisbury Plain, three geologically distinct hill ranges. The River Avon rises in the Cotswolds and initially follows the dip of those hills in an easterly direction. Unlike her sister streams, which continue eastwards to join the Thames, the Avon flows south through Malmesbury Vale, via Melksham, and then cuts back through the limestone strata of the 'geological Cotswolds' on its way to the Bristol Channel.

The River Biss, which springs up below the porous chalk strata of Salisbury Plain and which flows by Westbury and through Trowbridge, meets the Avon just up river from Bradford. Down from Bradford, the Avon is joined by the River Frome which rises in the eastern Mendips, and later by the Midford Brook, which is born of the Cam Brook and Wellow Brook, both of which flow from the Mendip foothills. These rivers and streams and their respective tributaries constituted an essential basis of the wool and cloth industries which have been such an important factor in the growth of the towns and villages in the area here described.

I had originally intended to consider the whole of the boundary where Somerset meets Wiltshire, extending farther south towards Mere in Wiltshire and Bruton in Somerset. However, the Longleat and Stourhead estates constitute a barrier to ramblers on the Wiltshire side and I felt that to include this extension southwards would expand the scope of the book to an unmanageable degree. Not only that, but there are sufficient variety and sources of interest in the area here defined, coupled with an historic unity represented by six hundred years of the wool and clothing trades to provide a suitable country for exploration.

WALKING IN THE COUNTRYSIDE

Walking, I am convinced, is the only way to truly appreciate the country-side. The great advantage of walking as a means of getting about the country is its complete flexibility. By that I mean you can go at the pace you choose and, providing you stick to rights of way, you can stop exactly where and when you wish, in order to examine some building or natural feature which presents itself, or simply to admire the view.

I always look forward to setting out on a country walk, and especially that moment when I step off the concrete highway and on to a grassy track or perhaps a field path. Quite suddenly the din and stink of the traffic dies down and the natural sounds take over: birdsong, the wind in the trees, the sound of your own footfall. Somehow it is a completely different world.

If we wish to walk, where can we do so? In the area where Somerset meets Wiltshire, there are a number of country lanes, green roads and field paths from which we can gain an inside view of the countryside. The ancient network of public footpaths and other rights of way is not as complete as it once was. The reason for this is quite simple. Before the age of motor transport, those who lived and worked on farms and in villages had usually to walk to get anywhere. Not that people went very far. Perhaps to the village church on a Sunday or to the nearest market town once a week to sell their produce.

A cursory glance at any large-scale Ordnance Survey map will reveal that the majority of footpaths and minor tracks provide shortcuts from farm to main road, from main road to village. Pedestrians always found the shortest route to suit their, as a rule, very local orbit, and it was natural that they should ignore lanes and roads when there was a shorter route across fields or between hedgerows. Many of these old ways became increasingly neglected in the period after the First World War when motor transport became more widespread. This tendency has been even more marked in the past twenty to thirty years. Former rights of way across agricultural land have sometimes been ploughed up and lost without trace, others that have been considered inconvenient or otherwise undesirable by farmers and landowners have been rendered inaccessible by some means or other. I have sometimes encountered public footpath notices which have been broken down, tracks between double hedgebanks which have had trees felled across them or mountains of rubbish dumped along their course. There are, too, problems presented in deciphering O.S. maps which have been rendered obsolete

11

when farmers bulldoze hedges to enlarge fields, or pipe streams underground to improve land drainage.

Yet one can understand the farmer's point of view. Gone are the days when he and his workers used the field paths; now that they no longer have any practical use, asks the farmer, why should ignorant townsfolk come and trample his crops. I have more than once been engaged in such a discussion with farmers after they had informed me that a public footpath no longer exists across their land and have been sent back the way I came. Yet what remains of our system of footpaths is surely worth maintaining. Some town and parish councils and local branches of the Ramblers' Association undertake the task of regularly walking all the rights of way in their areas so that local landowners cannot apply for their closure. There can surely be no objection to people using these footpaths providing they do so with respect for crops and observe the Country Code by closing gates and avoiding all risk of fire. In the long term, the farming community must stand to gain from an increased public awareness of the value of the countryside. It is a precious heritage which belongs to us all; it provides food for the spirit as well as the body.

A fairly substantial network of footpaths exists near the centres of population, for example around Frome and Bradford-on-Avon, and in the places generally recognised as beauty spots such as Vallis Vale and the Limpley Stoke valley. There are other areas, relatively far from towns and with unspectacular scenery such as the hinterland around Norton St Philip, where perhaps a majority of footpaths have disappeared or are unusable. Nevertheless, as partial compensation for the dearth of footpaths there are many miles of lanes and minor roads along which one encounters very little traffic and which provide suitable routes for walkers.

I have walked all the footpaths included here and I have also checked them out with the relevant County authorities as being still legally accessible as public rights of way. There are times when it is not easy to keep strictly to the public right of way, particularly when paths cross open fields which have been ploughed or which are waist high in corn. In such cases it is advisable to make a detour around the edge of the field in order to avoid trampling down crops or negotiating the ridge and furrow of a freshly ploughed field.

I am not one to go for a country ramble equipped as though I were planning to climb Everest but it should be remembered that, even in the driest weather, you are likely to encounter some mud and that, following a wet spell, it is as well to wear waterproof boots. Beware, too, of footpaths in the summer overgrown with brambles and stinging nettles — you will suffer greatly if you wear shorts!

Each of the walks described below is accompanied by an appropriate sketch map, to show the route taken and the main features to be seen. The maps together with the detailed description given should be sufficient to guide the rambler. However, anyone with a serious interest is recommended to acquire the relevant Ordnance Survey maps. These are as follows:

1:50,000 Series — 'Landranger': These maps have replaced the old 1 inch series and are drawn to a slightly larger scale. All public rights of way are shown in red.

    Sheet 172: Bristol and Bath
    Sheet 173: Swindon and Devizes
    Sheet 183: Yeovil and Frome
    Sheet 184: Salisbury and the Plain

1:25,000 Second Series — 'Pathfinder': These larger-scale maps have partially replaced the former 1:25,000 First Series. Their advantage over the First Series is that all public rights of way are shown in green, whereas no distinction was formerly made between footpaths and rights of way.

    Sheet ST65/75: Radstock and Wellow
    Sheet ST66/76: Bath
    Sheet ST86/96: Melksham

1:25,000 First Series: Each of the First Series maps only covers half the area included in the Second Series.

    Sheet ST85: Trowbridge
    Sheet ST74: Frome
    Sheet ST84: Warminster
    Sheet ST77: Marshfield
    Sheet ST95: Cheverell

Guide to Maps

The simplified maps accompanying the rambles in this book, together with the directions given in the text (in italics) will, I trust, provide a sufficient guide even to the inexperienced walker. I have, indeed, walked every inch described and in doing so have discovered those public footpaths which are no longer accessible as well as points where even the Ordnance Survey maps are misleading, if not inaccurate because dated.

The key to the maps is as follows:

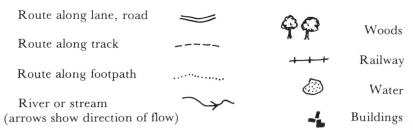

Route along lane, road

Route along track

Route along footpath

River or stream
(arrows show direction of flow)

Woods

Railway

Water

Buildings

13

Iford House and bridge

14

1 AVONCLIFF

via Freshford, Iford and Westwood

Distance: 3½ miles

THE WALK is a splendid one by the banks of the Rivers Avon and Frome through a peaceful and delicious countryside. The gorge-like valley at Avoncliff opens out downstream where the Avon is joined by the Frome. The valley from Freshford to Iford is open meadow in its lower reaches, but wooded on its upper slopes. The mellow stone of the bridge, manor house and Italianate gardens at Iford contrasts delightfully with the verdure of the valley. There is a steep hill to climb from Iford up to Westwood and from Upper Westwood down again to Avoncliff.

There are pubs at Avoncliff and Freshford and tea gardens at Avoncliff.

Avoncliff is reached by road from Bradford-on-Avon or Westwood. From Bradford you take the Belcombe Road which forks left to follow the railway. The road ends at Avoncliff where there is some parking space by the canal. From Upper Westwood there is a lane which leads steeply down to the canal.

Avoncliff is a small but diverse community. There are the remains of two mills, facing one another on the banks of the Avon, there has been much quarrying and mining of Bath Stone in the hillsides around Avoncliff and even today there is a stone mine close by at Upper Westwood. The Kennet and Avon Canal and the railway both pass through Avoncliff, the former here crosses the river and railway by a massive aqueduct, recently restored, and the railway even has a halt here. There is an old pub 'The Cross Guns' with a terrace which looks out onto the aqueduct and weir, and several houses scattered about the river, canal and railway. Access by road, however, is restricted, and only footpaths serve to reach points down river towards Freshford and up the hill opposite the pub to Turleigh and Winsley.

The mills formed part of the Hungerford Estate in the late fifteenth century and were used for grinding corn and fulling wool, though they were latterly employed as flock mills, finally closing down on the outbreak of the Second World War. 'The Old Court' is a surprising and attractive edifice consisting of a continuous group of three-storey buildings facing a courtyard on three sides. It was so named during the nineteen-twenties when used as a hotel. Before the First World War it housed the Bradford Union Workhouse though its origin predates the Poor Law Act. It was built around 1800; its original purpose is not clear but it is generally accepted that it had some connection with the cloth trade, possibly comprising weavers' workshops and accommodation. There is a domed drying house still standing behind the main building.

To begin the walk, make for the footpath which passes under the aqueduct, in the same direction as the flow of the river, on the pub side. You pass by the Old Court on the left and continue by a well-worn footpath which is hedged on both sides and slightly elevated above the meadow beside the river on the right.

You reach a stile which takes you into a meadow — the path now follows a course close by the river. Traverse the meadow until you reach a stile where the hanging woods sweep down to the river bank. This stile also marks the point where we leave Wiltshire to enter Somerset (officially Avon). The woods soon end at a kissing gate where you enter a field — here you follow the worn footpath across the field towards Freshford Bridge and 'The Inn' to the right. The river which flows under Freshford Bridge is the Frome; the Frome joins the Avon just before the railway viaduct below.

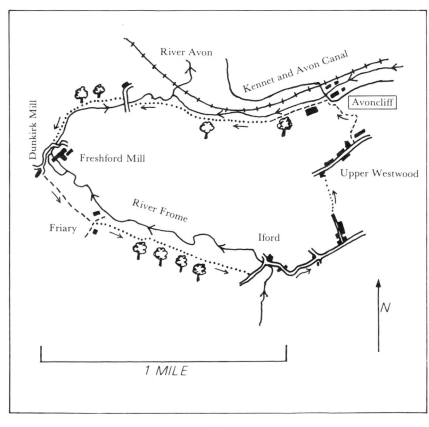

Cross Freshford Bridge and enter a field on the left by a kissing gate to follow a signposted public footpath. After about fifty yards the right of way ascends the wooded slope on the right. Follow the footpath up the hill fairly steeply until you reach a kissing gate. If you bear right here you reach Freshford village, which is worth exploring. But to continue the walk, bear left down the hill again towards the river. The hillside here slopes fairly precipitously and there is an old iron fence to protect the walker for the first section. You eventually descend to the level of the river and leave the woods to enter a field by a stile. Carry on in the same direction towards the mills ahead and cross another stile to reach the lane.

Freshford Mill was originally the property of Hinton Charterhouse Priory and, after the dissolution, fell into the hands of a Trowbridge clothier. It continued as a cloth mill, and latterly as a flock mill, under various owners and tenants, until the Second World War. After the war it was bought by Peradin which still occupies it as a base for the manufacture of rubber products.

Follow the lane beside the river and take the first turning on the left towards Dunkirk Mill.

Dunkirk Mill dates from the eighteenth century and, after standing empty since 1912, has recently been converted into a dwelling house.

Opposite the main entrance to Dunkirk Mill is a track crossing a field between fences. Follow this track to a tiny settlement in a cleft reaching down to the valley known as Friary (here were sited quarters for the lay brothers from nearby Hinton Priory). Cross a brook by a plank bridge, then bear a few steps left before continuing in the same direction towards a gate. Enter a field and cross it by the left-hand edge towards a gate in the woods opposite. After a couple of hundred yards the right of way bears left down to the meadow. You now bear right and enjoy an unimpeded stretch of field path before reaching the lane at Iford. Bear left to cross the bridge to Iford Manor.

Iford Manor has an attractive early-eighteenth-century front, though parts of the house are much older. The buildings on the left, with the fine oriel window, are the former stables, now converted into a pair of cottages. The gardens, with cloisters and colonnade and many fragments of ancient sculpture collected mainly from Italy, are quite unexpected along this quiet stretch of the River Frome.

Iford Manor is listed in the Domesday Book; it was purchased by Sir Thomas Hungerford in 1369, whose family held it for three centuries. In 1899 Iford was acquired by the architect Harold Peto, who set about creating his unique garden on this favourable south-facing slope. The gardens are regularly open in the summer months, when a booklet on the Manor and Gardens is available.

The picturesque Iford Bridge is of medieval origin and is supposed to have been built by the Carthusian monks from Hinton Charterhouse around 1400; Mr Peto erected the figure of Britannia.

Bear right at Iford Manor up the rather steep hill by the lane towards Westwood. You reach the road by the gatehouse to Iford. Bear right and then left into the modern estate ironically named 'The Pastures'. Bear left at the bottom beside the bungalow by a metalled pathway which leads to a stile and then to the lane which runs through Upper Westwood.

Bear right past a former chapel beside the road and a large house called Greenhill (interesting because its eighteenth-century façade is flanked on either side by low gabled wings of the previous century — the whole perfectly symmetrical) towards a terrace of two-storey houses with long front gardens. Just before this terrace bear left by the pavement on the right and past the entrance to Westwood Stone Mine. Follow the footpath straight on and then as it bears to the right down the hill to Avoncliff. You encounter various crosstracks but simply keep to the most obvious, direct path until you emerge at the lane which brings you out just above the canal aqueduct.

AVONCLIFF

2   BECKINGTON

via Rode, Woolverton, Laverton and Lullington

Distance: 5½ miles

THE WALK passes through five villages of varied size and interest. Most of the walking is by field paths although there is a stretch of lane between Woolverton and Laverton. An ancient track takes you west from Rode to cross the River Frome by Scutt's Bridge, a former packhorse bridge, unwidened and accessible only on foot, like the bridge at Tellisford, a little farther down river.

The cross-country walking between villages will surely convince you that there really is no better way to appreciate a rural landscape than on foot. At the time of writing there existed not a single public footpath sign on this route, and the way is rendered difficult in places by fences of barbed wire and fallen trees. How reassuring it is to discover, in such circumstances, old stiles, kissing gates and footbridges over streams which confirm the existence of ancient rights of way.

There are pubs at Beckington, Rode and Woolverton; Laverton and Lullington are publess. Scutt's Bridge makes a pleasant spot for a picnic.

Beckington may be familiar to many who live in the district where Somerset meets Wiltshire as a large village lying astride the junction of two main roads: the A36 Bath–Warminster and the A361 Frome–Trowbridge roads. A perambulation of Beckington is well worth the effort: it has a rich store of old stone houses and an interesting church.

Make for Church Hill, the entrance to which can be found just behind the Woolpack Inn in the centre of the village, where the Warminster Road meets the village main street. It is usually possible to park somewhere in Church Hill.

St George's Church stands handsomely in its churchyard, a short distance from the street, and its most impressive feature — a fine Norman tower — at once captures your attention. Unfortunately, Beckington church is usually kept locked but the interior has much of interest. There are several monuments, including one on the west wall to Samuel Daniel the poet, who died in 1619. There is a piscina, a timbered roof above clerestory windows and several fine corbel heads.

If you wish to see more of Beckington before setting out on the circular walk, bear left as you leave the churchyard gate and walk on to Beckington Castle, a three-storied, sixteenth-century mansion with three gables facing the street and a castellated porch and stair turret at the side. Bear right here by the former main road (now a cul de sac) and right again at the present road. Opposite is the entrance to Stubbs Lane where the conical roof of a little gazebo marks the boundary wall of Beckington House, a three-gabled house set back from the road. Cross the road and bear left. Just below is a most attractive Baptist Chapel dated 1786 and beyond that, on the same side, a former coaching inn, now a private house, where the iron support of the inn's name board still projects from the wall.

Back on the main road you can see The Grange and Beckington Abbey on the opposite side, parts of which date from the sixteenth century — these buildings have ecclesiastical origins though details are obscure. Continue through the village, past many old and attractive houses. Beckington is a sizeable village and its many substantial houses bear witness to a former prosperity founded on the wool trade.

Baptist Chapel, Beckington

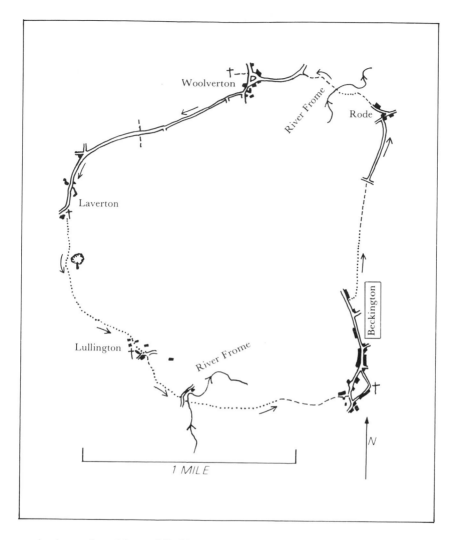

1 MILE

N

At the northern fringe of Beckington you reach a road junction with the road to Trowbridge to the right. Continue northwards here, past the village hall and playground. Just before the row of houses ahead cross a stile on the right which leads into a field. Once past the gardens of these houses head for a wooden stile in the bottom left corner. Follow the hedgerow on your right. Cross a stone stile and continue to follow the hedgerow until a kissing gate leads you on to a track between hedgebanks. The appearance of dumped rubbish heralds the proximity of a lane ahead. Continue straight on towards Rode. The River Frome flows unseen in the shallow valley to your left; the church spire at Woolverton can be seen above the far bank.

Bear right on reaching the southern limits of Rode, then sharp left. Once past the houses on your right, the road abruptly reverts to a tree-lined track and leads down towards the River Frome. Look out for a stile on your left.

21

Before crossing this stile it is worth inspecting the fallen masonry and disused channels just ahead. You can see the stone-lined walls of a former mill leat which supplied the Rockabella clothing factory which once occupied the site.

Cross the stile and bear right, following the course of the former mill stream on the right, until you reach the narrow, three-arched packhorse bridge, known as Scutt's Bridge, across the River Frome.

Just up river from Scutt's Bridge, a single-span stone bridge crosses a mill stream which at this point returns to the river, having been diverted to supply the former Scuttsbridge Mill, now demolished.

Cross Scutt's Bridge and continue by the track ahead. Bear left at the lane and walk on into Woolverton. Woolverton church is set back from the main road and, while of no especial interest, is attractive enough in its flowery, walled churchyard.

On leaving the church, bear right at the main road, then right again for the lane to Laverton. After about half a mile there is a crosstrack, the northern section of which represents a short piece of the Poole–Bath Roman road; the southern section is the old Henhambridge Way.

Take the left fork ahead and descend to Laverton which has its own church, St Mary's, but which is really little more than a hamlet. Leave the road and walk through the churchyard to the far side. Cross the fence into a yard between farm buildings. Continue forward, bearing a little to the right, until you reach a gate at the top corner of a field on the far side of the buildings. The right of way here actually crosses the field to reach a stile and footbridge across the stream at the bottom. Depending upon the season and what is growing in the field may encourage you to follow the field boundary on the left towards the stream and then along the bottom beside the stream towards the stile. In any event, cross the single stone slab footbridge and bear right. The field narrows where it meets a wood on the left. The path steepens as it enters the wood briefly to emerge into a field.

Now follow the hedgebank on your right until it swings a little way to the left. Here enter the next field and head for the small pond ahead, marked by a clump of trees. Cross the stile beyond — now Lullington comes into view. Make for a point a little to the left of the church. Once past a barn, bear right past the farmhouse and church.

Lullington is a most attractive small village with a gem of a Norman church at its centre. All Saints has a splendid northern doorway which can easily be missed if you do not walk right round the church but merely enter by the south door. The plan of the church is unusual in that the tower is in the centre, between the nave and chancel. Inside, the columns at the four corners of the tower are very elaborate and make a fascinating study. The church also contains an inscribed and much decorated Norman font. Lullington village is quiet and well preserved although the school is now a house and there is neither shop nor pub. The sinuous lines of the cottages facing the green are more reminiscent of South Devon than Wiltshire.

Norman north doorway at All Saints Church, Lullington

Walk past the church, then left past the thatched cottages and sharp right down a track. Just before the house ahead bear right to cross a stream and follow the trees on the left.

Some authorities* believe that the ridges in the ground here indicate that this path follows the course of the Poole–Bath Roman road, which connects with the fragment already seen north of the lane between Woolverton and Laverton.

Now bear a little to the left to cross the driveway to Orchardleigh House and follow the boundary of the estate until you find a stile in the bottom left corner. Cross the lane and enter the field opposite. Make for the modern footbridge ahead and cross the River Frome. Head straight across the field towards a gate opposite. The path now diverges: do not head for the farm ahead but bear slightly to the right to climb the field obliquely to the far right corner. Cross into the next field and walk straight ahead until you reach the farm track. This leads you into Stubbs Lane and Beckington, almost opposite Church Street.

LULLINGTON

---

*Bernard BERRY, *A Lost Roman Road,* George Allen and Unwin, 1963.

3 BRATTON CASTLE

via Upton Cow Down and Old Dilton

Distance: 7½ miles

THE WALK is a longish but exhilarating one. The path from Bratton Castle along the chalk scarp is exposed and windswept and the bare downs afford little protection against the elements. It is advisable to choose a clear, sunny day for this walk as the views are far and wide. Bratton Castle is an impressive Iron Age hill fort which encloses a long barrow of the Bronze Age. It is pretty certain that the Battle of Ethundun, described in the Anglo Saxon Chronicle as the battle at which King Alfred defeated the Danes, took place near here, by the village of Edington which lies under the scarp to the north east. Tradition has it that the White Horse was cut to commemorate the great victory, though a more accurate date for its origin is probably the early eighteenth century. The redundant and unique church at Old Dilton provides a haven of rest after the stiff walk across open hills.

Bratton Castle may be approached by road from Bratton village or from Westbury. In either case park under the south-facing ramparts.

The double bank and ditch of the Castle's southern perimeter are well preserved and of impressive proportions. It is worth scaling the ramparts to reach the enclosure which contains in its 25 acres a rather mutilated long barrow. The western perimeter of the Castle leads to the scarp edge and the Westbury White Horse. The angle of the chalk scarp here is relatively steep and reaches down through the chalk and greensand strata directly to the clay vale.

To begin the walk, make for the metalled track which runs along the top of the scarp away from Bratton Castle and in a south-westerly direction. At the crossroads carry straight on.

Immediately on the left is the entrance to a chalk quarry. Here chalk is removed to provide one of the raw materials for the cement works situated below the Castle. You can get a good view of the enormous hole in the chalk from the track a little farther on. The vertical walls of the quarry give an excellent cross section through the near horizontal chalk strata,

25

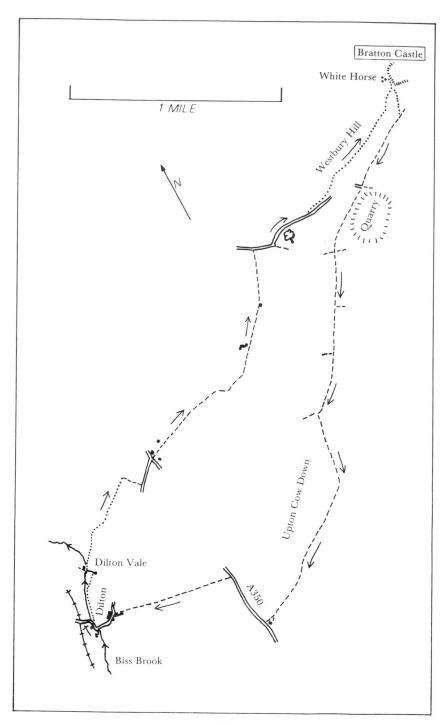

Bratton Castle

White Horse

Westbury Hill

Quarry

1 MILE

N

Upton Cow Down

Dilton Vale

Dilton

A350

Biss Brook

distinguished by lines of flint nodules. The quarried chalk is crushed and mixed with water and the resultant slurry is pumped by underground pipeline to the nearby factory. Here the chalk is mixed with clay which is dug from the ground adjacent to the works; the mixture is then baked in kilns to make cement.

Continue along the high, straight track. You pass first one, and then two, tracks which lead downhill to the right. At the third junction, as you are approaching the summit of Upton Cow Down, do not bear right and down the scarp, but go straight on.

There are firing ranges within earshot to the left and official notices warning of the danger of same. However, the track ahead is a designated right of way and some distance from the rat-tat-tat of gunfire.

Shortly after the junction you gradually descend from around 650 feet to 400 feet at the barn near the main road below. Ahead lies the village of Upton Scudamore with the unmistakable eminence of Cley Hill beyond. Leave the path by bearing right at the barn to reach the road. By doing so you avoid walking along the busy main road but also miss an interesting little guidepost on the roadside dated 1840. Cross the main road, bear right and, rather than risking the road, take the old grass track which runs for a short distance above and beside the main road. This old way surely represents the former course of the road. Where this track descends to the modern road there is, conveniently, a grass verge by which you can continue in safety to the signposted bridleway which bears off to the left towards Dilton Farm.

This bridleway crosses wide open fields on the Lower Chalk which here forms a kind of level terrace between the Middle and Upper Chalk of Upton Cow Down and the Greensand ridge beyond. As you drop down to the lane between the farm buildings you can see that the wall of the barn opposite is built of stone blocks from the greensand.

Bear left at Dilton Farm down the lane which leads past houses and across a bridge over the infant Biss Brook to St Mary's Church, whose low roof line and bell turret stand cheek by jowl with the railway bridge and embankment behind.

St Mary's was declared redundant in 1973 and is now maintained under the Redundant Churches Fund. The perpendicular exterior, with its bell turret and variety of windows, leads to an even more unexpected interior. The nave and north aisle contain an entirely unspoilt eighteenth-century interior where every available space has been utilised for the erection of box pews, some of which incorporate medieval pews and parts of a former screen. Above all rises a grand three-decker pulpit complete with sounding board. There is a gallery under the bell turret and a larger one, which was once used as a schoolroom with access from outside, over the vestry. There is very little else to distract the visitor from the sight of scrubbed timber and creamy Bath Stone pillars set against whitewashed walls and ceiling; all serve to make this old church distinct and fascinating.

St Mary's Church, Old Dilton

28

From the church, turn back to the bridge and bear left, over the stile, where a signposted public footpath takes you along the edge of a field with the boundary on your left. A small field is fenced off ahead: do not enter this field but bear slightly to the right, keeping the fence on your left, and make for the farm buildings ahead. Bear left at the track and then right, over a stile, with the farmhouse and its garden on your left. Cross another stile where a stream meets the one you have been following from Old Dilton. At this point the waters divide into a mill leat which flows away to your right whilst the main body of the stream continues on your left.

You now leave the waters of the valley and climb directly up the hillside ahead. At the summit you pass through a squeeze belly stile and follow the field boundary on your right. Cross a second stile to enter a field boundary on your right and again follow the field boundary ahead until you reach a crosstrack. The bungaloid sprawl of Westbury Leigh is visible to the left; bear right down to the lane and then left to reach the main road. Cross the road and continue by Wellhead Drove. This lane leads past a few houses on your left, beside fields on your right, to woods ahead. Ignore a track leading uphill to the right and carry on until you reach a junction marked by a small brick building belonging to the local water authority. Here bear left along a wide track which can be very muddy after rain.

The beech wood and dell on your left marks the boundary between the Upper Greensand and the Lower Chalk: the path now takes you on to the Lower Chalk, which again forms a terrace below the chalk scarp on your right.

As you reach the road you will see the White Horse looming up ahead. Bear right at the road and, once past the woods on either side, look out for a sign indicating a public foothpath leading across fields towards the White Horse and Bratton Castle.

Once out of the cultivated fields by a stile you will find a stone direction marker on the crest of the scarp. The height above sea level is 754 feet and, on a clear day, you can spend time finding all the landmarks indicated, and a few more besides.

4 BUCKLAND DINHAM

via Orchardleigh, Spring Gardens and Elliots

Distance: 4½ miles

THE WALK is an easy one through delightful country. There are field paths, tracks through woods, hills with distant views, a country estate, ancient churches, streams and footbridges, and riverside meadows: an albeit unspectacular but nevertheless very appealing slice of rural Somerset. Apart from Buckland Dinham there are no pubs or shops on the route.

Buckland Dinham is an attractive village on a spur of land about three miles north west of Frome. It was once a centre for the cloth trade. The church of St Michael and All Angels is found a short distance uphill from the main road which passes through the village. Interesting features include an elaborate perpendicular tower and a doorway and two windows of the Norman period. Inside there is a Norman font, a Lady Chapel on the south which has been restored this century and a north chapel which contains two effigies — a knight and his lady. These figures represent the donor Sir John Dinham, who died in 1332, and his wife. The original Dinham was Oliver de Dinant who held the manor in 1205 and hailed from Dinan in Brittany.

Facing the church from the approach road bear right along the signposted public footpath. Follow the wall on the right until you reach a stile. Cross the stile and enter a field which slopes away down towards Buckland Brook. Cross the field to reach a wooden footbridge in the bottom left corner, then make for a steel-framed footbridge. Cross the next field diagonally towards a stile in the bottom left corner, then make for the gate straight ahead and follow the hedgebank and wood on the left up to the top left corner of this last field.

Cross the stile and continue in the same direction along a roughly worn track through woods, first passing on the left a netted enclosure, then a stand of pine, then a cottage away to the right. Carry on until you reach a stile within sight of a metalled drive. Keep walking in a straight line until you reach the drive. Follow the drive through Orchardleigh Estate until you reach some buildings on the right. Here you bear right along a track which is signposted 'To the Church'. (You may wish to press on a little way along the drive to gain a view of Orchardleigh House which dates from the nineteenth century and is a riot of architectural styles.)

The lane to the church takes you through one gate and then another after which you bear left and pass through some iron gates to the small and ancient church of St Mary. It stands on an island at the head of Orchardleigh Lake and is reached by a footbridge.

Orchardleigh church consists only of nave, chancel, bellcote and north chapel. Notable features are the priest's door, piscina and aumbry and especially the various carved heads, including two either side of the sanctuary which formerly supported the lenten veil, and the stained glass. The church survived the Reformation fairly intact and was sympathetically restored in 1879. Most of the carved heads and much of the stained glass is medieval and it is a fascinating exercise to view all these representations of the human face and pick out which are Victorian and which medieval. The difference of five or six centuries is quite striking and I leave it to the reader to make his own observations.

From the church door head across the field towards the stone marker. The fragment of shaped stone here marks the site of the old manor house which was demolished in 1856. The ground can be seen to be very uneven: a sure sign of vanished buildings.

From the stone marker climb up the hill with the sunken wall and hedgerow on the right, towards a stile at the top right corner. Look behind for a view of Orchardleigh House on the slope of the hill opposite and the lake below. Cross the stile and continue with the hedgebank on the right.

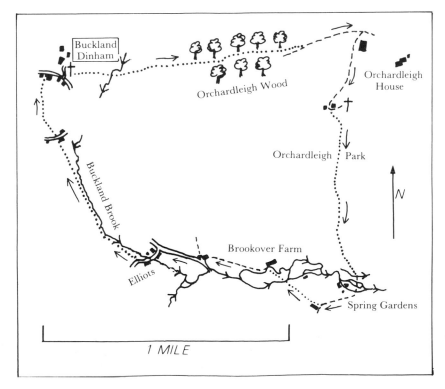

As you crest the hill (known as 'The Down') you will enjoy an extensive view: to the east the Westbury White Horse, to the south east Cley Hill, then the wooded hills of Longleat with the town of Frome in the foreground.

Cross the stile in the top right-hand corner and follow a rough but well marked path downhill, bear left at a footpath T-junction and left again where the path forks. You then emerge into a field where you follow the right of way directly downhill towards a gap in the hedge after which you follow the hedgebank on the left.

You eventually reach a gate beyond which is a stone bridge. The old bridge has two arches and a cutwater and, according to the O.S. map, once crossed a leat which supplied water meadows a little farther down the valley; the water has now ceased to flow.

Follow the lane ahead to cross three more bridges over flowing water. The restored and converted Spring Gardens Mill can be seen away to your right. Take the track just before you reach a group of buildings on the right side of the lane. Do not follow the track to the house below but carry straight on across the field ahead, to the right of the projecting hedgerow. Continue in a straight line towards the tree-lined stream beyond. About twenty yards to the left of a sluice gate through which you will hear water rushing, there is a stone footbridge.

Cross the bridge and head across the field towards another footbridge to the left of the farm buildings. Now bear left along the access road from Brookover Farm to the main road. You reach the main road at a point where an entrance gateway to the Orchardleigh Estate is flanked by lodges.

Bear right up the main road for a short distance before turning left down a minor road through the hamlet known as Elliots. Once past the buildings look out for a stone stile under a massive beech tree. Leave the lane here and head down across the field towards a wooden stile opposite. You now follow a very pleasant field path beside the Buckland Brook towards Buckland Dinham.

As you enter the last field before the houses on the lower slope of the hill ahead, make for a gap between the houses. Here you will find a large stone stile which drops you into a lane. The field path continues directly opposite. In this field, head for a kissing gate in the top left corner, then follow the hedgebank on the right, and cross three more stiles before reaching houses. Simply continue in the same direction until you reach the main road through the village. At the main road bear right and then first left to reach the church.

When I visited the church at Buckland Dinham I had a strange experience. It was a gloomy Sunday afternoon when I entered the church, and as the door slammed shut behind me I stepped into the nave and felt there was someone else in the church. I instinctively looked towards the chancel and saw a figure, in the shape of an aged cleric of an earlier century — an old, wizened man dressed in black and holding a Bible. He stood beside the choir stalls and stared intently at me. He seemed neither hostile nor friendly but looked at me as though I had interrupted him. I was somewhat taken aback and looked away for a moment. When I looked back he was gone and I realised I had seen a ghost (and I am certainly not one given to seeing ghosts).

Orchardleigh had a poet attached to it when Henry Newbolt married one

Late-thirteenth-century piscina at Orchardleigh Church

of the Duckworths and, indeed, there is a memorial tablet to Newbolt on the nave wall of St Mary's Church. In one of his poems* Newbolt relates the story of the squire of Orchardleigh who, on his deathbed, asked for his dog Fidele, who had once saved his life, to be buried at his feet in the family chapel. This was done, but when the Bishop of Bath and Wells heard that a dog had been buried in church he ordered that the parson remove Fidele to the churchyard beside the lake. The sexton was given instructions but could not bring himself to disturb Fidele. In the words of Henry Newbolt:

> The grave was dug; the mason came
> And carved on stone Fidele's name;
> But the dog that the Sexton laid inside
> Was a dog that never had lived or died.
>
> So the Parson was praised, and the scandal stayed,
> Till, a long time after, the church decayed,
> And, laying the floor anew, they found
> In the tomb of the Squire the bones of a hound.

ORCHARDLEIGH

*The poem is 'Fidele's Grassy Tomb', from: Henry NEWBOLT, *Collected Poems, 1897–1907*, Thomas Nelson.

5 CLAVERTON

via Bathampton Down

Distance: 5½ miles

THE WALK is an exhilarating one which includes a trek around Bathampton Down with its magnificent views over Bath and the hills beyond, Lansdown, Little Solsbury Hill, Charmy Down, Banner Down and Bathford Hill. All these hills are essentially composed of the near horizontal strata of Great Oolitic Limestone, commonly known as Bath Stone and once much worked in this locality as a source of excellent building stone. Indeed, there are many signs of quarrying activity to be seen in the perambulation of Bathampton Down.

The ascent of Bathampton Down is by lane from Claverton and entails a steady climb over about half a mile. The descent to the Kennet and Avon Canal is considerably steeper and the section of the walk along the towpath of the canal can be very muddy after wet weather. There are no pubs anywhere on this walk but Bathampton Down provides a choice of picnic sites, so long as you are careful not to obstruct the golf course.

Claverton (the name means the farm where burdock grows) is a linear village on the lower slopes of Bathampton Down arranged along a street which runs parallel to the main road a short distance below. In the centre are some attractive terraces enclosed by stone walls; these are all that remain of the old manor house, which dated from the late sixteenth century. The house was rebuilt in the early eighteenth century much higher up the hill with commanding views across the valley of the River Avon. Claverton Manor now houses the American Museum, so that the public has access to the house and grounds.

St Mary's Church may be reached by a footpath from the street through the village. The church was heavily restored in the mid-nineteenth century and is unusual in that the chancel seems to be as long as the nave. The church contains a striking monument to Sir William Bassett (died 1613) and his wife. This is in the form of life-size sculptures of the couple brightly painted and set upright in niches in the side of the chancel. Outside there is a good example of a scratch dial on the porch and, in the churchyard, Ralph Allen's mausoleum crowned with a great stone pyramid. Ralph Allen was a great friend of Richard Graves who was rector of Claverton for fifty-five years. In the churchyard also are the graves of four of Cromwell's soldiers who were killed in action nearby in 1643, Claverton Manor having been captured by the Parliamentary General, Sir William Waller.

With your back to the church bear right past some houses until you reach the lane. Bear right and begin the ascent of Bathampton Down. The lane swings first to the left, then to the right: the woods on the right are in the grounds of Claverton Manor, the valley below to the left forms a steep and narrow cleft in the Down in which Vineyard Farm is situated.

You pass the entrance to Claverton Manor (the American Museum) and, when the lane begins to level out, you pass a signposted Private Car Park which belongs to the Museum. A few yards past the entrance to the car park, in the stone wall on the right, there is a stile in the form of projecting stone steps. Climb the wall here and bear slightly to the right to follow the field boundary on the right. As you cross another interesting stile, you will see a signpost in the field beyond indicating that this piece of land is known as Bushey Norwood, and belongs to the National Trust. Bath University is the group of modern buildings to the left.

The right of way follows the field boundary on the right-hand side towards a kissing gate in the far right-hand corner about half a mile beyond.

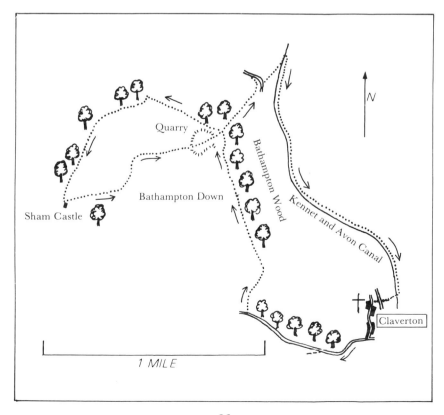

Stile at Bushey Norwood

You may be intrigued by the many large stones scattered around the field, some of which are set on end in a rather unnatural way. Bathampton Down, like Little Solsbury Hill, a little to the north, was used by the natives before Roman times for cultivation and settlement. These upright stones are mere stones which were erected to define field boundaries.

The kissing gate leads you along a footpath which is far from straight and not always clear. You are somewhat below the summit of the down; there is higher ground to the left and the hillside falls away steeply to the right. There is much evidence of former quarrying activity in the shape of numerous mounds and hollows. To follow the right of way you should simply stick to the most well used path which keeps you on a fairly even contour. The woods become thicker until you reach a crosstrack. Bear left up the hill. After a short distance the path emerges into the open: here you bear sharp right towards a stile. Cross the stile and head straight on towards the trees — simply follow what appears to be the path worn by use until you emerge into the open on the slopes of Bathampton Down which face north towards Batheaston. You now follow the right of way in the same direction you took through the woods, i.e. towards Bath or, more immediately, towards the trees on the far side of the open field. As you approach these trees, head for a corner of the woods which projects into the field towards you.

You now make your way ahead below the trees on your right and under the mast on your left. Notice a number of tumuli in the hillside to your left. Continue to follow the edge of the woods on your right towards a stile, past the buildings belonging to Bath Golf Club and on towards the Sham Castle.

Sham Castle, an artificial ruin, was built by Ralph Allen, to beautify the view from his townhouse in North Parade in Bath, Prior Park having not yet been built. It seems amazing to the twentieth-century mind that anyone should want to build an artificial ruin, but perhaps even more surprising that the eighteenth-century love of order should demand that the Sham Castle's façade be absolutely symmetrical. But whoever heard of a symmetrical ruin?

To continue the walk, follow the track which leads gently uphill to the left of Sham Castle towards the summit of Bathampton Down. At the edge of a clump of trees on your right you must cross the fairway of the golf course towards a gap in the linear earthwork ahead. Pass through the gap and follow the embankment on the left.

Bathampton Down was certainly the site of a pre-Roman settlement as the tumuli and evidence of Iron Age agriculture testify. It is likely that the linear earthwork here was built to protect the original Iron Age enclosure. Some authorities refer to the earthwork as part of the post-Roman Wansdyke and its form, a simple ditch and north-facing bank, and its position in relation to the east and west sections of the Wansdyke, would seem to support this view.

Continue to follow the embankment as far as a T-junction marked by a pair of public footpath signs pointing left and right. Go straight across towards the summit of the hill opposite: below and beyond this high point you will see the remains of a former quarry. This is not a dangerous site, however, as there is no sheer drop to the bottom level.

Before moving on from this high point it is worth taking a final view of the landscape. There is a panorama stretching from the Georgian terraces of Bath strung and stacked on the slopes of Lansdown in the west, to Brown's Folly standing above the thick woods of Bathford Hill to the east. Between these there is the limestone plateau of this southern fringe of the Cotswolds dissected into isolated masses by rivers and streams, including the River Avon, Lam Brook, St Catherine's Brook and By Brook. The Fosse Way runs straight from Bath north eastwards to Batheaston and is then forced to deflect rather in order to ascend Banner Down on whose summit it resumes its characteristic straight course, but now in a more northerly direction, in order to avoid meeting the steep-sided valley of the By Brook.

The Celtic field system of Bathampton Down can be seen well from this point too. Looking down on the north-facing slope, the outlines of small rectangular fields are visible although the laying out of a golf course with greens and bunkers and trees has not helped.

Mere stones, Bushey Norwood

Make your way to the bottom of the quarry and walk along the excavated hollow towards the exit where you begin to descend by the steep, straight track which you earlier partly ascended: you now follow this track to the main road far below.

You may notice some large blocks of stone marked with deep grooves embedded in this track. These are most likely the old stone sleeper blocks in which the iron rails of the tramway serving the quarry were set. This inclined plane system consisted of two lines — one by which loaded wagons descended by a rope and another by which empty wagons ascended.

At the main road, cross over and bear right. Look for a public footpath on the left — here cross the stile and continue down to the canal. There is a footbridge across the canal here. Cross over and bear right along the towpath which you follow for about one and a half miles to Claverton. As you approach a point below the village you will see a bridge over the canal. Cross the bridge and follow the track — look out for a stile on the right which affords a short-cut to the main road and thence to the village street below the church.

CLAVERTON

6 CLEY HILL

via Corsley, Corsley Heath and the Whitbournes

Distance: 6½ miles

THE WALK includes a number of field paths, tracks and lanes. Just inside the county, the country traversed has a definite Wiltshire feel about it, with spacious fields and wide vistas on the slopes of Cley Hill, although some writers note that the isolated knoll of Cley Hill reminds them more of Somerset and the similarly abrupt and solitary hills which occur in and around the flat and low-lying Sedgemoor.

You descend the Upper Greensand scarp to Corsley and ascend it towards Corsley Heath. The Whitbournes are situated in a cleft in the greensand which forms an attractive little valley between the ridge of Corsley Heath and the wooded hills of Longleat Estate. This longish and somewhat energetic walk can be adapted, but walking along the busy A362 should be avoided if possible. There are pubs at Corsley and Corsley Heath.

Cley Hill belongs to the National Trust and can be approached from the A362; a car park is provided. The view from the summit is well worth the climb; the illustrator of this book managed to locate his house in Bradford-on-Avon from here with the aid of a telescope.

To begin the walk, head downhill from Cley Hill car park along the approach road towards a crosstrack about 150 yards above the main road. Here bear left along a deeply sunken and somewhat overgrown track. After about a quarter of a mile the track diverges. Here you bear left up to the edge of a field. Bear right and follow the field boundary on the right for a little over half a mile until you reach a track. This track leads up to the main road. However, you bear left here and simply follow this well-marked way towards the north-eastern spur of Cley Hill where you enter the edge of Norridge Wood.

The track now reverts to a path through the wood which soon emerges at a gate through which you enter the field beyond. From here you can see Cley Hill Farm below and, beyond, the ridge on which the long, linear village of Chapmanslade is situated.

Follow the footpath downhill beside the field boundary on the left — you pass through a gate to reach a metalled lane which you follow until you reach a crossroads. Bear right and begin to descend the greensand ridge past the house aptly named 'Sandhayes' (= sandy fields) until you reach Corsley church.

41

The Manor Farmhouse beside the church is a large, gabled house with mullioned and transomed windows and is, unusually, built of brick. The original house was built by Sir John Thynne in the 1550s and he lived here while he was working on Longleat. The church is nineteenth century and is usually kept locked; sheep are employed to keep the churchyard grass cropped. The little school opposite the church still serves the surrounding community.

From the church take the lane towards Corsley Heath. Once past the Cross Keys Inn the road forks. Take the right fork but bear sharp left up a track to the left of some farm buildings. At the end of the track cross into the field on the left and head across the field and up the slope towards the row of houses on the crest of the hill ahead. Leave the field by a gate and follow the lane to the main road ahead.

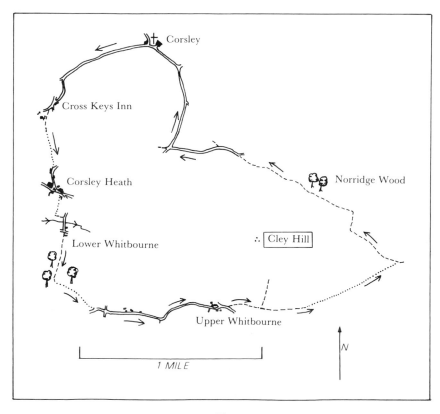

Corsley Church and Cley Hill

Bear left at the main road and cross over towards the cottages set back from the road on the far side. Look out for a stile just before you reach the cottages. Cross into a field and follow the hedgebank on the left-hand side towards a stile. Cross the stile and bear left along the lane, then right and straight on at the crossroads to climb the hill beyond by an unmetalled track.

You soon reach woods on your right and, when the track begins to level out, look for a stile on the left. Cross into a field and head towards a stile in the top right-hand corner, then over another stile ahead. Follow the field boundary on the left until you reach a stile in the top corner where you drop down into a sunken track which takes you down to a crossroads. To the right is an entrance gate to Longleat. However, carry on by the lane ahead towards Upper Whitbourne and the Frome – Warminster road.

Fortunately, you only have to negotiate a few yards of the main road before you bear left up a sunken way. This takes you to the crosstrack and approach road to the car park below Cley Hill.

7 COMBE HAY

via Odd Down and Southstoke

Distance: 4 miles

THE WALK comprises an easy half day's ramble with no steep slopes. The route includes lanes, tracks, field paths, the Wansdyke and sight of the Fosse Way. There are pubs at Combe Hay and Southstoke.

Combe Hay is a straggling village built on a south-facing slope which looks down towards the Cam Brook. The village church, which has a small perpendicular tower, is at the south end of the village, rather hidden behind the trees of the churchyard and close by Combe Hay Manor. If you venture beyond the semicircular apse at the east end of the church you can see over the church wall the east façade of the manor house. The house is eighteenth century, partly *c.* 1730 and partly *c.* 1770. The east façade, in sight here, is strictly classical, and very restrained. The Bath Stone used is particularly honey coloured and is most attractive in the morning sun. The church is fairly undistinguished, having been much restored in the last century. Notice the stables which face the church across the churchyard; these Pevsner dates at *c.* 1700.

From the church turn left up the hill. At the crossroads bear right along the lane signposted to Bath.

Notice the wall of engineering bricks immediately on the right. This forms the head of a tunnel of the old, disused Camerton branch railway line. If you look over the wall you can see the cutting; the line was tunnelled under the road junction at this point. The house to the left is named 'Tunnel Farm House'.

At the fork ahead bear right and pass the cottage on the right called 'Three Days'. The considerable range of apparently derelict buildings on the slope to your left is Week Farm. A littl· farther on you pass Fortnight Farm on your left. Beyond this the track deteriorates rather. At a point where the track swings to the right there is a gate and stile which lead into a sloping field. The O.S. map indicates a right of way across here to the trees ahead. However, since the disappearance of former field boundaries has rendered the course of the footpath indistinguishable across this arable land, it is advisable to continue on the stony track, first swinging right, then left where another track joins from the right.

45

Near the summit you can see, on your left, a sunken way which marks the end of the footpath whose start we found at the stile below. It is worth descending this path, through the trees, to the edge of the field. Here you can rest and enjoy the splendid view down the cleft in which Fortnight and Week Farms are situated. Beyond them is the valley of the Cam Brook and, beyond it, the ridge which separates the Cam and Wellow Brooks.

At the junction of tracks and lanes above, walk straight on along the metalled road towards Odd Down. The land on the left has been excavated whilst beyond are the rooftops of Bath's southern fringe. Past St Gregory's School look for an iron gate and stile on the right.

Before passing through the stile notice the name of the road which crosses at the junction ahead: 'The Old Fosse Road'. The modern road here follows the course of the Roman road before it descends to the ancient spa.

Through the stile you follow the level path flanked by houses, playing fields and agricultural fields. You are now traversing the plateau-like summit of Odd Down.

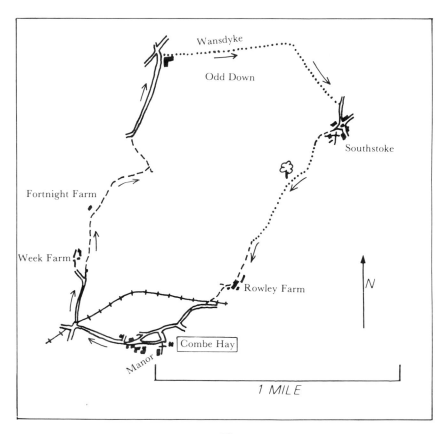

Week Farm, near Combe Hay

47

This path is on the bank of the Wansdyke, which in parts can be seen to be a good ten feet above the level of the land to the north. The Wansdyke is a linear earthwork and occurs in two distinct parts, the East and West Wansdyke. The East Wansdyke runs across the Marlborough Downs whilst the West Wansdyke runs in an east–west direction south of Bristol and Bath, of which this section across Odd Down is a part. The Wansdyke consists of a single bank with a ditch on the northern side, thereby implying that it was built by a people living on the south side in defence against an enemy to the north. It is probable, therefore, that it was built by the Britons, under the command of Ambrosius and his lieutenant Arthur, against the Saxons.

Continue along the footpath until you reach a stone wall on your right which marks a field boundary. Climb over the wooden stile here and follow the stone wall towards the trees ahead. Leaving the field, you cross a concreted track and pass through an iron kissing gate. Carry on through the trees until the path drops down into a lane. Bear right here and follow the lane down into Southstoke.

The little village green, marked by white railings and a bench seat, is a good spot to rest before the second leg of the walk back to Combe Hay. Alternatively, you may seek refreshment at the 'Packhorse' pub, which is by the road below the green. This interesting pub has a seventeenth-century three-gabled façade and an unspoilt interior which is worth seeing.

From the green bear right, past the church, farm and barn. Immediately past the barn the lane forks: take the left fork downhill. A little way down, as the lane bends to the left, there is an iron stile on the right. Pass through here and head downhill across the field towards a tree which marks the left corner of the wood below. From here follow the footpath downhill, pass through two iron stiles, keeping the wood on your right. Soon you pass a derelict house on your left. Keep descending, in the same general direction, down to the stream. Cross the stream. The footpath now climbs the hill opposite, keeping the wood on the left, until you reach a double stile in the hedge above. Cross into a field and strike a path diagonally across this field towards a point about halfway along the hedgebank on the right-hand edge of the field. You will see the rooftops of Rowley Farm a little beyond. Cross the stile and bear left along a fenced way past Rowley Farm. Beyond the farmhouse you will see the tower of Combe Hay church directly ahead. Take the left fork here to head downhill. The entrance drive to Caisson House is on the left.

It was here that the famous caisson lock was built on the Somerset Coal Canal. Directly opposite this drive you can see a short stretch of the canal, now dry, but unmistakable nevertheless. Just before you reach the road, you will pass by a brick wall like the one at Tunnel Farm House. This marks another railway tunnel — a peer over the top will reveal the old cutting.

Bear right at the lane and gradually descend into the village.

8 DUNDAS AQUEDUCT

via Conkwell, Farleigh Wick and Warleigh

Distance: 4 miles

THE WALK is almost entirely by field paths and green tracks and includes a lovely section of the River Avon and Limpley Stoke valley. This is a quiet and peaceful walk through meadows and woods and across hillsides with magnificent views.

There is adequate parking near the Dundas Aqueduct in a layby on the A36 about a quarter of a mile beyond the Viaduct Inn and on the right as you drive towards Claverton. The canal can be reached from either end of the layby: a footpath leads down from the Claverton end and a track from the other end.

The wide basin here marks the junction of the Kennet and Avon Canal, now restored, and the old Somerset Coal Canal, which here began its course towards the Somerset Coalfield. At the time of writing, there are plans to restore the first quarter mile of the old coal canal to provide moorings for craft using the Kennet and Avon. Some of the stonework of the old canal can be seen in the garden of the house beside the canal basin.

Cross the canal by the bridge beyond the old crane, then cross the aqueduct, a massive and rather magnificent three-arched bridge which here carries the canal across both the railway and the river.

Once you have reached the far bank, keep walking straight ahead, to the left of the single-storey workshop and over a stile marked 'Public Path'. Shortly after the stile you will see a minor path leading away to the left and up to a gap in the trees where there is a stile leading into a field. You head diagonally across this field towards the far left corner of the wood opposite. Cross the stile here and continue by bearing right to follow a steep, sunken and stone-strewn track up the hill towards Conkwell.

You emerge into the hamlet of Conkwell at the bottom of its single street at Spring Cottage; the spring can be seen in the hillside in front of the cottage. Other houses also tell a story in their names: there is Cromwell's Rest, where Oliver Cromwell is said to have rested between military engagements (it is also said that his men poisoned all the wells in the vicinity except that at Conkwell), and Old Bounds Cottage, which marks the

Somerset–Wiltshire boundary. Looking back on Conkwell from the top of its one street puts me in mind of a Cornish fishing village where the cottages are stacked steeply in a narrow cleft leading down to the sea.

Bear left at the top of the village and straight on at the T-junction ahead. Shortly past the junction, look out for a stone stile on the left which leads into a field and to a footpath along the edge of a wood, which you continue to follow through three more fields. In the fourth you bear right at the field boundary ahead and then left into a field which is almost completely surrounded by woods. Follow the path along the right-hand boundary towards a gate ahead. Do not pass through this gate but bear right towards a further gate. Now bear left and follow the wood on the left towards a gate by which you enter the wood.

You soon emerge into a field: follow the boundary on the left, first beside a wood, then beside the boundary wall of Inwoods House. Look for a gate ahead on the left: enter a yard by this gate and bear right past the buildings to find the drive towards the main road, Farleigh Wick and the Fox and Hounds.

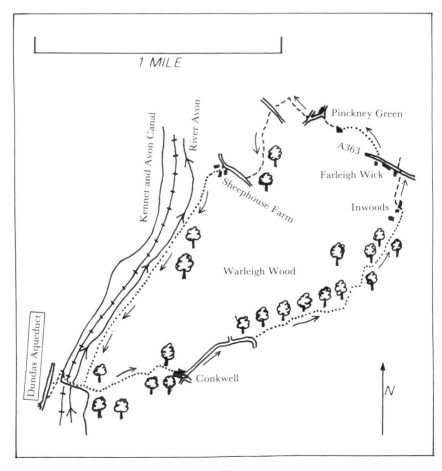

50

Crane and canal basin at Dundas Aqueduct

Once past the pub, cross the road and enter the field opposite by a stile. The right of way crosses the field diagonally towards a kissing gate by the buildings ahead. Continue towards Pinckney Green, a small settlement consisting mainly of former quarrymen's cottages. Bear left at the T-junction and walk up to the lane. On the far side is a green track signposted as a public footpath. Follow this path towards a left-hand bend where you begin to descend past a house towards an arch above which the main road passes. Once through the arch the track narrows: follow the footpath downhill towards woods. You suddenly emerge at the top of a field which affords a splendid view down to the River Avon and across the valley towards Claverton.

Continue by this footpath until you meet a track coming from the left. Follow this way downhill until you meet a lane. Bear right to reach Sheephouse Farm on the left. Bear left, not towards the farmhouse, but towards the buildings to the right of the house. Bear right into the farmyard and pass through a gate to follow a rough track which gradually descends to the riverside footpath. You now follow the river for best part of a mile towards Dundas Aqueduct.

Shortly before you reach the aqueduct you pass by a prominent ridge, like a low railway embankment which stops just short of the river in order to allow space for the footpath. This ridge once carried a tramway down from stone quarries in the hillside below Conkwell and bridged the river to reach a quay on the Kennet and Avon Canal opposite.

Head towards the stile at the rear of the boathouse ahead and make your way up the rough path to the canal above; from here you retrace your steps at the start of the walk back to the layby on the main road.

9 HOLT

via Great Chalfield, Little Chalfield and Bradford Leigh

Distance: 4 miles

THE WALK is an easy one, using well-trodden paths, with no steep slopes. The route includes the medieval manor house of Great Chalfield. There are several pubs in Holt and tea gardens at Little Chalfield.

The most attractive part of Holt is around the village green, or Ham Green, as it is known. This is the starting point for the walk.

Take the minor road which leads away from Ham Green towards the south east. You soon reach the Parish Church of St Katherine.

The church, with the exception of the tower and entrance to the south porch, was entirely rebuilt in 1891, but in medieval Gothic style.

Bear left, past the church, by a track which leads to a kissing gate and a footpath through a field.

The grounds of The Courts are on the left. The seven acres of gardens are owned by the National Trust and are open to the public in the summer months, although the house, which has an eighteenth-century façade, is not.

Pass through a squeezebelly stile and bear left to reach the main road through the village at the entrance of The Courts.

Before crossing the road notice the United Reformed Church buildings on the left: the older, plainer structure behind with the pointed windows and hipped roof dates from 1810.

Cross the road, pass Holt Village Hall (ex Holt Reading Rooms 1873, according to a stone set in the wall), and walk along the road called 'The Midlands'. Bear right at Beaven's Leather Works (established 1770) and walk past a number of old industrial buildings of brick and stone.

Look out for a surprise: beneath a wall at right angles to the road is an old pump set in the bricked-up entrance to a former well-house. The entrance is denoted by a pair of Tuscan columns surmounted by a straight entablature. Below the stone is the following inscription: 'Sacred to the memory of Lady Lisle and the Revd. James Lewis, the persons who patronised this spring and rendered it famous in the year 1720.' This pump marks the site of a former spa which once rivalled Bath.

Once past Sawtell's Bedding Factory bear left along a track and enter a field by a stile. Continue straight ahead, between hedgebanks as the field narrows. Cross the brook below by a stile and head across the next field, bearing slightly to the right until you reach a stile in the hedgebank at the top which drops you into the next field. Follow the hedgebank on the right, past a copse and over a stile. Great Chalfield and the Mill Cottages are now visible to the left.

Cross the brook below by a wooden bridge and head across the next field to find the exit into the lane at the top left-hand corner, just above the Mill Cottages. Follow the lane beside the moat and fortified boundary wall, past the diminutive All Saints Church and magnificent fifteenth-century manor house, which belongs to the National Trust, and is open to the public on Wednesday afternoons in the summer.

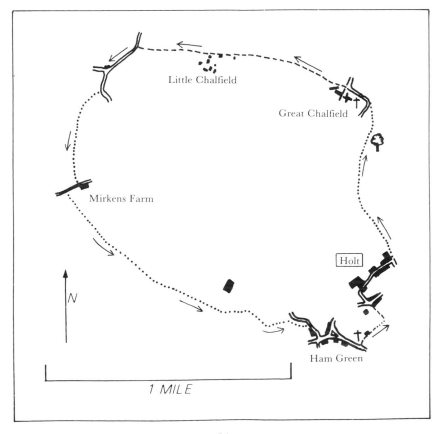

Little Chalfield

Great Chalfield

Mirkens Farm

Holt

N

Ham Green

1 MILE

Pump at Holt spa

There is so much worth seeing in this late medieval manor house, in the church and the grounds that it would be futile to attempt a full description here. The house was built by Thomas Tropnell in the late fifteenth century when he acquired the manor. He also enlarged the church, parts of which date from the thirteenth century. The centre of the house opens into a great hall, which was converted into rooms on different levels when the house was let to tenant farmers at a later date. The house was thoroughly restored at the beginning of the present century, thanks to some very detailed drawings that were made in 1837, before the alterations.

Continue past Great Chalfield along the lane signposted 'Private Road to Home Farm'. Once past the farm buildings, carry on along a fenced track between fields to Little Chalfield. Walk on along an avenue of beech and chestnut trees and bear left at the lane ahead. Once over the stream in the valley bottom here bear right into a field and follow the hedgebank on your left.

You emerge into a lane at Mirkens Farm where you bear right towards Bradford Leigh. Bear left along a track just past the first house on the left. This leads directly into a field — here you follow the hedgebank on the left. You can see the spire of Christchurch in Bradford-on-Avon away to your right. Keep straight on towards the hedgebank at the top of the field. Enter the next field by the gate and follow the hedgebank on the left, where the following field is reached at the bottom left-hand corner. Head to the left of the pylon and follow the hedgebank on the right.

The next field is reached by an iron gate. Follow the hedgebank on the right — you can see a group of farm buildings on the left side of the field. At the bottom of this field bear left and look for a gap in the hedge by which you reach the next field. Head diagonally across this field — you can see Holt beyond. Cross the ditch below and head towards the bottom left corner of the next field. Bear left here along the hedgebank — this will lead you back to Ham Green via South Wraxall Road.

'About three miles from Bradford, is the little village of Holt, more famous for its medicinal waters than for any other peculiarity . . . The Holt-water is esteemed as being a powerful alternative, and many instances of its having cured the most virulent scrophula are recorded.'

from Britton's *Beauties of Wiltshire c.* 1800.

10   LIMPLEY STOKE

via Midford, Pipehouse and Hinton Priory

Distance: 4½ miles

THE WALK provides a variety of scenery and much of interest. There is a steep descent from Limpley Stoke to the Midford Brook and a gentler ascent from Midford to Pipehouse Lane. This is a pleasant, easy ramble which could well provide a whole day's walk, with a break for refreshment at, say, Midford, where there is a pub, or perhaps including a visit to Hinton Priory.

The starting point for this walk is Limpley Stoke parish church. The lane outside the church is too narrow for parking a car and it is therefore necessary to park a little distance away.

St Mary's Church is set high on a hill on the southern edge of Limpley Stoke, far removed from the village centre. It is an ancient church, as the Saxon arch (once a doorway) in the arcade testifies. We are told that behind the oak panelling in the chancel are to be found Roman tiles laid in a herring-bone pattern, the tiles having been rescued from a Roman settlement sited nearby. We are also told that the nave walls are believed to be those of a small chapel built in 1001 to mark the boundary of land given by Ethelred, son of King Edgar, to the Abbess of Shaftesbury in 973. Shaftesbury Abbey became the richest Abbey in England and was given the Manor of Bradford in 1001. Before the creation of Avon, the boundary between Somerset and Wiltshire, as well as that between the parishes of Limpley Stoke (in Wiltshire) and Freshford (in Somerset), passed through the field immediately behind the church.

St Mary's is a small, simple and unrestored church. It has a low, plain, unbuttressed tower surmounted by a short spire, partly hidden behind a parapet. The porch is early thirteenth century with a round-headed arch and a statue of the madonna and child looking out of a niche above the door. Inside, in addition to the plain and narrow Saxon arch, there is a fine stone pulpit built into the north wall, Jacobean panelling on the balcony of the gallery and a font whose bowl is believed to be of Saxon origin.

On leaving the church, bear left along Church Lane, cross Warminster Road and continue along Midford Lane. Go straight on until you reach a forked turning where you bear right along a lane signposted 'Old Track'. Quite soon, the road bears right towards more houses. Go straight ahead by the unmetalled track, to the left of a bungalow named 'Chatleys'.

The track begins to descend, at first gently, then more steeply. At the crosstrack below bear right, then sharp left and continue to descend to the valley bottom. There are some good views from here towards Monkton Combe and the course of the old Camerton Branch Railway can be traced where it cuts into the opposite slope.

As you reach the river you will see the old mills straight ahead; these can be reached by a footpath which crosses the island lying between Midford Brook and the mill stream. Bear left here over a stile before the footbridge and follow the riverside footpath. You soon pass a dilapidated weir.

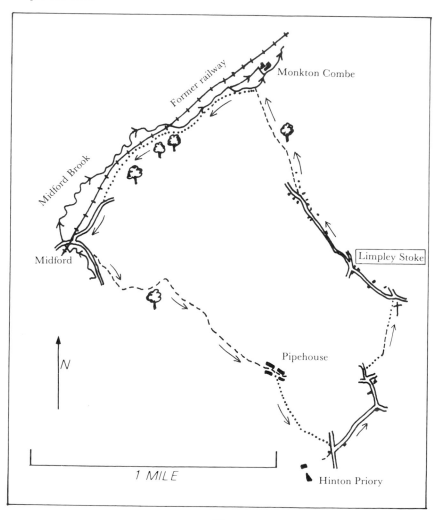

Follow the river for about half a mile until you reach the brick piers of the former
railway bridge which carried the railway from the north to the south bank. You now leave
the Midford Brook and follow the railway embankment on your right. You soon reach a
cutting through the embankment which provides a view north westwards towards
Tucking Mill. However, there is no right of way through the cutting: continue the walk
by keeping the railway embankment on your right-hand side. To do this necessitates
crossing two low barbed-wire fences which section of a small area of boggy ground where
marsh marigolds grow. Once over the second line of barbed wire the way ahead is clear.
You pass through a gap in a stone wall into a field; from here you press on with the old
railway a little below on your right.

Notice Midford Castle on the crest of the hill opposite. This unique
complex of buildings dates from the late eighteenth century; the group
includes a gatehouse, stables, chapel and summer house, while the main
house is in the form of a triangle, with circular towers at each corner.
According to an old guide book, the reason for this curious plan is as follows:
'A well known society gambler once made a fortune at the card tables by
turning up the ace of clubs; in the hopes of perpetuating his good luck, he
built this residence.'*

The exit from this field is in the far left corner where you cross a stile and drop down
into Midford Lane, the same lane you left for Old Track at Limpley Stoke.

Follow Midford Lane down to the main road below. Bear left and look for the
beginning of an unmetalled track a hundred yards or so along on the left. Take this old
sunken way and follow it uphill for about a mile. Soon after the track levels out you reach
houses at the hamlet of Pipehouse. Just past the former 'Village Room 1903' (now a
house), look for a stile on the right. Cross this stile, then soon cross another and enter a
field by a gate. Cross this field, keeping the farm buildings on your left, towards the stile
in the far boundary.

You can now see the buildings at Hinton Priory straight ahead. It is
possible to get some good views of the Priory and chapel by following the
right of way which passes by the back of the complex. Our route, however,
follows the footpath which reaches the main road near the entrance to
Hinton Priory.

Bear slightly left towards the far left corner of the next field, then over a stile and
leftwards again to reach the stile which faces the main road a little way before the
gatehouse.

Hinton Priory is a ruin of a former Carthusian priory founded in 1232
and abandoned at the dissolution of the monasteries some three centuries
later. The remains are scanty compared to the great ruined abbeys of the
North of England, but they make an interesting study nonetheless, and may
be visited on Wednesdays on application to the gatehouse on the main road.
The chapter house, sacristy, refectory and a small portion of the church and
*B. F. HARRISON, *By the By-Ways Around Bristol,* Partridge and Love, 1927.

St Mary's Church, Limpley Stoke

cloisters are visible, as well as the outline of the cloisters, which measure 226 feet square. The nearby village of Hinton Charterhouse commemorates the Carthusian connection in its name, and the Priory owned much land in the area.

From Hinton Priory take Abbey Lane, directly opposite the gatehouse. Once past the entrance to Homewood Park Hotel you can see Limpley Stoke church ahead. You begin to descend before the lane bears left; ignore the lane to the right and at the crossroads below go straight ahead. After a few yards you will find an indicated public footpath on the right. Cross the stone stile, follow the lane until it bears right and then keep to the footpath which continues straight ahead. There are two stiles and two fields more to cross before reaching Limpley Stoke church.

TRACK BELOW PIPEHOUSE

11 NORTON ST PHILIP

via Hinton Charterhouse

Distance: 4 miles

THE WALK is a pleasant and varied one which could provide an enjoyable half day's ramble or even a whole day. There are one or two excellent spots for a picnic as well as a choice of pubs at both Norton St Philip and Hinton Charterhouse. There are also tea rooms at Norton.

The route leaves Norton by a field path and thence by a quiet lane through a delightfully unspoilt valley, then towards a wood where it follows a track up a hillside. Now the route traverses a plateau at around 400 feet with wide views north and south for almost a mile before reaching Hinton Charterhouse. From Hinton church field paths are followed for over a mile back to Norton St Philip.

Norton St Philip is best known for The George Inn, that magnificent hostelry at the centre of the village which must have been photographed and sketched a million times. The George is said to have been built by the monks of Hinton Charterhouse and there is certainly much of an ecclesiastical style about the detailing of the door and windows of the stone-built ground floor. The inn was certainly used as a centre for the cloth trade; the top storey was a great hall for the buying and selling of wool and cloth. The George has its associations with the famous too. Oliver Cromwell slept here when in pursuit of Charles II; the Duke of Monmouth stayed over on his ill-fated expedition — he was actually shot at through the window of his room at the inn. Last but not least, Samuel Pepys ate and slept here and he records his satisfaction at doing so in his diary. The George Inn is a fascinating old building and it is well worth exploring the ground floor to which the pub user has access.

The view from the back of the George, where there is a garden, is worth seeing. The ground slopes down to a cricket pitch on Church Mead and beyond that is the church of St Philip and St James with its singular tower, said by some to have been constructed from fragments of the ruined priory at Hinton Charterhouse. There is a path on the right-hand side of the inn (as you face it) which leads down across Church Mead towards the church. Norton St Philip is a sizeable village which retains its shops and school (still in its original building of 1827 — opposite the church). There are many attractive, stone-built houses and the pavements are made up of irregular stone flags.

To begin the walk, face The George Inn and bear right. Take the left fork downhill and then bear sharp right. This is North Street, although there does not seem to be any indication of this. At the end of North Street bear left along a lane leading downhill. Look out for a pair of wooden stiles on the right just before Lyde Green Cottage. Cross these to enter a field and walk straight across towards a gate in the hedgerow on the far side. Cross into the next field and follow the field boundary on the left to reach a stile in the far corner just above the lane. Now head downhill towards a stile which drops you into the lane.

Bear right and continue along the lane for about a mile. Eventually you will pass, on your left, a footbridge and ford across a stream. Keep to the lane here but look out for a gate on the right-hand side about a hundred yards farther on. This gate bears a notice which informs you that beyond is a private wood and that you must keep to the footpath. Find your way on to the footpath through a gap to the left of the gate and follow the well-marked path, actually more of a track, up the hillside.

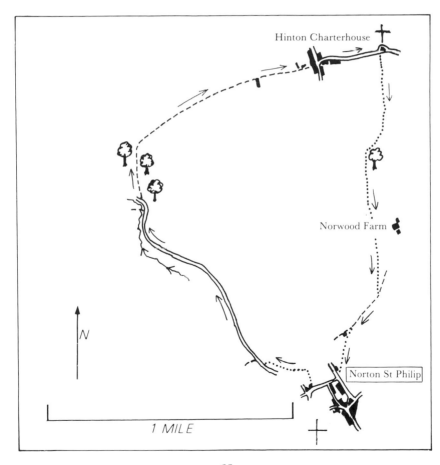

Footpath beside The George Inn, Norton St Philip

After a while you leave the woods to enter a clearing: this is a peaceful spot with fine views. Bear right here and leave the clearing at the top right corner. From here the track climbs a little farther and then reaches a level path between cornfields leading across a plateau towards Hinton Charterhouse. At Hinton you cross the main road and continue by the lane opposite towards Hinton church.

The next stage of the route is indicated by a public footpath sign leading across a stile on the right-hand side, just before Hinton church is reached. Enter the field and head towards the next stile by an oak tree. You now progress along the fenced boundary towards a stile at the end. From here you head straight across the field ahead towards a stile in the far hedgerow. Now bear slightly to the right and, at the copse ahead (actually a disused and overgrown sandpit), bear right. Follow the edge of the copse on your left and, when you emerge at a field, bear slightly left just to the left of the nearest pylon and to the right of the wood. Again you carry straight on, now towards a stile in the field boundary a little to the right of a small farm building. Then follow the field boundary on the right towards a gate and the access road to the farm which you passed on your left.

Follow this lane for a short distance, keeping an eye open for a stile at the top of the bank on the left: this is found about twenty yards before the cottage. Cross into a field and bear right towards the stile beside the cottage. Head diagonally across the next field towards a stile in the bottom left corner: this drops you into the road at the northern edge of Norton St Philip. Bear left to reach the village centre.

12 NUNNEY

via Lower Whatley, Egford, Vallis Vale, Great Elm and Whatley

Distance: 7 miles

Alternative shorter route: 2 miles

THE WALK includes some very pretty footpaths beside streams and some exhilarating stretches across fields. Unfortunately, there is no footpath between Lower Whatley and Egford and you are left with no alternative but to use the road for a little over a mile. This minor road provides a pleasant view over the valley of the Nunney Brook, although your enjoyment may be marred by the large trucks which serve the nearby quarries. Consequently, this walk is perhaps best reserved for the weekend, when the quarries are presumably quiet. There are pubs at Nunney and Whatley.

In addition, a much shorter walk is suggested which avoids this stretch of road walking.

Nunney is a gem of a village, by-passed by the main road, its buildings charmingly grouped around the brook which flows openly towards the moat of Nunney Castle. The castle itself is surprising in being built where it is — not in some defendable, hill-top position but sitting low in a valley with a village about it. The castle is a ruin, but its four massive towers and curtain walls are pretty well intact, and the whole blends in remarkably well with the rest of the village and far from dominates the scene.

All Saints Church, opposite the castle, has a more commanding position than the castle; it is situated on a gentle slope overlooking the village. The church contains much of the thirteenth and fourteenth centuries; perhaps its most notable features are the monuments to be seen in the north aisle. They consist of a knight and lady of the fifteenth century and another couple of the Elizabethan period. There is also a fourteenth-century knight lying on the windowsill behind. These stone sculptures provide an interesting study of evolving fashion in armour, dress and hairstyles.

From Nunney Castle and church, walk downstream beside Nunney Brook and take the first turning on the left towards Combe Farm. As you approach the farmhouse bear right over a stile and into a field beside the brook. Now head down to the little stone bridge

66

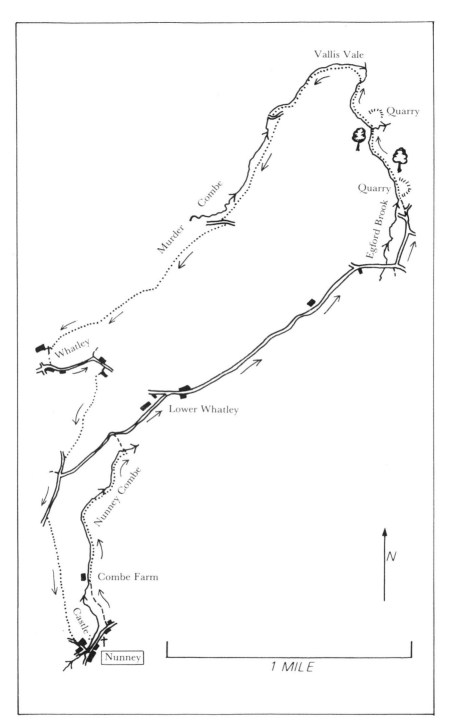

Vallis Vale

Quarry

Quarry

Murder   Combe

Egford Brook

Whatley

Lower Whatley

Nunney Combe

Combe Farm

Castle

Nunney

N

1 MILE

*which spans Nunney Brook and follow the footpath along the stream's right-hand bank
for a little over a mile.*

*The waters begin to flow much more slowly as you approach a weir by a footbridge.
Cross the footbridge and climb up to a minor road. Bear right through Lower Whatley
and continue by way of the road for about a mile to Egford. Once past Egford Farm, the
road crosses Nunney Brook (now Egford Brook) and a mill leat. Now you bear left; soon
a lane joins from the right and your road swings uphill to the left. At this point head
straight on along a track towards Vallis Farm. Look for a stile beside a gate on the left;
cross the stile and follow the footpath beside the stream.*

You soon pass by a large, abandoned quarry on your right where you can
see the tilted and folded strata of Carboniferous Limestone which in parts is
stained yellow from the overlying Jurassic strata.

*As you cross a bridge you will see, beyond an enormous heap of Mendip stone
chippings, another outcrop of rock marking another former quarry. This site exhibits to
perfection the horizontal Jurassic strata lying unconformably on the tilted Carboniferous
rocks.*

*From here you can either walk along the bed of the old railway track which left the
main line just above Hapsford Bridge to run along Vallis Vale and Murder Combe to
serve Whatley Quarry, or you can stick to the footpath beside the stream. If you follow the
streamside footpath you will notice that the direction of the flow is now against you,
rather than with you. This is not the Egford Brook, but the waters which flow from
Murder Combe and Wadbury Valley and which unite at Great Elm, a little upstream. A
little way along the footpath there is an old lime kiln which is still pretty well intact. The
top of the kiln projects several feet over the base of the hopper where the burnt lime was
extracted. The footpath soon joins the former railway track and crosses the stream. You
now follow the course of the old railway under a bridge beside the stream.*

*You soon pass under a new bridge which carries the railway, from a tunnel in the hill
on your left, across the stream and into a tunnel through the hill on the opposite bank.
This modern section of the railway line represents a rerouting of the branch line serving
Whatley Quarry.*

*Follow the track of the old railway beside the stream until you reach the road below
Great Elm. Do not cross the road to continue but bear left, up the hill, and look out for a
gap in the trees on the right where the right of way is indicated by a post bearing a public
footpath sign and an arrow pointing to Murder Combe. This is an enjoyable stretch
along the edge of the wood-clad valley with views over the quarried slopes towards the
wooded hill on which the Iron Age Tedbury Camp is sited.*

*The footpath emerges at a road between two enormous Mendip stone boulders. Here
you bear left for a short distance before continuing along footpaths by turning right
between hedgebanks. These soon revert to a single field boundary which you follow on
your left. As you reach the bottom left-hand corner of this field you cross into the next field
to follow the hedgebank on your right.*

*You will see the spire of Whatley church ahead and feel assured that you are heading
straight towards it. Your progress may be interrupted by the sound of blasting emanating
from the huge quarry on the far side of the valley to your right. There is a wide view,*

Quarry showing unconformity in Vallis Vale

especially to the south east, where you can see the plateau on which Frome is built and, beyond Frome, you can see Cley Hill and the forested hills of Longleat.

Follow the hedgebank on the right until you reach the top right-hand corner of the field where you cross over a barbed-wire fence into the adjoining field. Bear left towards the church. The big house before the church is the old rectory and there is a ha-ha between the house's garden and the cow field, that is, a sunken wall and ditch which ensures that the view from the house and garden is unimpaired but confines beasts to the fields. Also notice the many irregular bumps and hollows in the corner of the field below the rectory; this surely marks the site of a lost village.

Cross the field below the church and head towards a gate in the churchyard wall. This gate is past opening and has to be climbed.

Most of St George's Church is the work of the Victorian restorers, although there are traces of the original thirteenth- and fourteenth-century work. The church is generally kept locked. Close by the church is Manor Farm which has seventeenth-century mullioned windows. The gatehouse, with decorated arch, is older still.

Nunney Castle and moat, north side

Leave the church by the main gateway to the road and bear left. Follow the road towards The Sun Inn public house and leave the road by the lane on the right past the pub towards the house beyond. Here cross the stile to the right of the house into the field; you now follow a field path for about half a mile. The former field boundaries here have been obliterated but you can easily find your direction by heading just to the right of the two dead elm trees ahead. Beyond these you will reach a field boundary in the corner of which there is an old iron kissing gate. Once through here you follow the line of trees ahead towards the road at the top corner of the field. There is an old wooden stile in the hedgebank just before you reach the extremity of this field but it is so overgrown that you are forced to cross the barbed-wire fence a little farther on.

You now follow the road for a few hundred yards until the next section of field path is reached. This is found where a track leads away left from the road and down towards Nunney Brook. Do not descend here but enter the field on the left past the track. You now head directly for the centre of Nunney which is about half a mile ahead: the castle with its massive round towers is most prominent.

Walk diagonally across the field until the far boundary comes into view; the stile will be found just to the right of an ash tree. Head straight across the next field, with Combe Farm to the left, towards a wooden stile. You now follow a well-marked footpath into the village.

Alternative short walk via Nunney Brook: If your intention is simply to sample the delights of Nunney and then enjoy a quiet country ramble in its environs, the following short walk is suggested.

Follow the walk as described along Nunney Brook as far as the point at which you emerge on to the road at Lower Whatley towards Egford. Here bear left and left again until you resume the walk as given above via field paths for the remaining half mile back to Nunney.

13 RODE

via Tellisford

Distance: 5 ½ miles
Alternative shorter route: 3 miles

THE WALK begins in the attractive village of Rode which itself is worth exploring. From the village centre the walk makes for the old church of St Laurence, at the southern periphery of the village and on the busy A361. From here the walk follows field paths for about half a mile to Monkley Lane, then the main road is followed for about 200 yards before turning down a quiet lane towards Vagg's Hill and Tellisford. This is an uneventful stretch but satisfying enough for those who enjoy rambling through quiet country.

An alternative and much more direct route to Tellisford is described; this follows a track from Rode down towards Scutts Bridge, a riverside path towards Langham House,* a track from there to the site of the former Langham Mill on the River Frome and thence by a riverside path to Tellisford Bridge. This is an attractive short walk.

Tellisford is publess but makes an ideal spot for a picnic. On reaching Tellisford Bridge, both routes unite and continue by lane to the village church and back down to Rode Bridge, where there is more evidence of former cloth mills.

The A361, although it passes close to St Laurence Church, by-passes the village, as does the B3109 to Bradford-on-Avon. The old village lies on land which slopes gently down to the River Frome. There is usually a parking place in the vicinity of the small, triangular village green, with a war memorial at its centre.

The prospect of rows of old stone houses from here is an enticing one and you may like to start the walk with a short perambulation of Rode itself. To do so, head towards the village centre. Notice the old Baptist Chapel, dated 1780, and adjacent school room, dated 1839. Farther on, past two pubs which stand opposite each other, in the vicinity of some old industrial buildings and set back from the street on the left, is an old Methodist Chapel, dated 1809. You can return to the village green by the lower street through the village by taking the left fork at the pubs.

*Langham House was formerly Rode Hill House, the scene of a notorious murder in Victorian times. The story is recounted in a recent book:
Bernard TAYLOR, *Cruelly Murdered,* Souvenir Press, 1979.

To start the walk take Church Lane which leads uphill from the village towards the A361 and St Laurence Church, which is usually kept unlocked and may be visited.

St Laurence dates from the fourteenth century although it has been heavily restored by the Victorians. The clerestory windows and arcading render it a light and airy building. There is an interesting painting on display of the village men holding hands and dancing in a circle round the church. This ancient custom apparently had pagan origins. Known as 'clipping the church', it was enacted on Shrove Tuesday night for the avowed purpose of driving out the devil, and survived in many parts of Wessex until the nineteenth century.

On leaving the church, turn right along the road towards the Bell Inn. Fortunately there is a pavement here, first on one side of the road, then the other. Directly opposite the Bell Inn cross a stile into a narrow field between two bungalows. Carry straight on and cross the next stile.

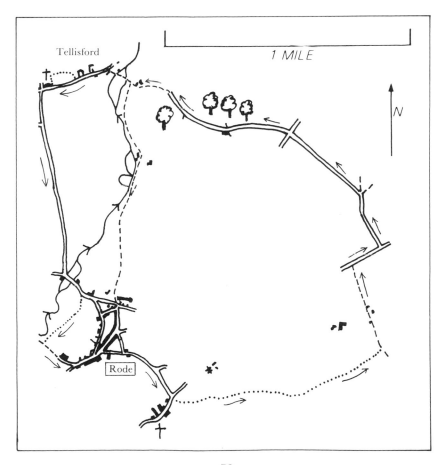

Away to the right you can see Seymour's Court, a fine old house which can only be appreciated from Rudge Lane on the opposite side.

Head straight across the next field to a stile in the hedge opposite. Follow the crooked hedgebank of the next field with Parsonage Farm to your left below. Cross into another field and walk past the barn ahead towards the top right-hand corner where the field narrows. Similarly, in the following field, make for the top right-hand corner and cross into a field in which you follow the ditch and hedgebank on your left. You soon cross into one last field which is much larger than the others. You continue to head in the same direction; an aid to navigation here is to make straight for the pylon ahead. As you approach the pylon you leave the field at a left-hand corner and drop down into Monkley Lane, which is no more than an unmetalled and somewhat overgrown track. Bear left here and head towards the main road.

Turn right at the main road for about 200 yards before turning left down a lane which marks the Somerset–Wiltshire boundary. Continue along this lane for a little over half a mile until you cross the B3109 to Bradford. The country here is more interesting as you approach Vagg's Hill, with woods to your right and splendid views down to the Frome and across the hill to Tellisford. As the lane descends it narrows before reaching the ancient packhorse bridge across the Frome.

First mention of Tellisford Mill was in 1574, when it was held by a clothing family from Trowbridge from the Hungerfords of Farleigh Castle. The mill, which is situated on the far side of the bridge, is now in ruins, but the mill stream still flows strongly and noisily through the ruined buildings.

Once over the bridge, walk past the old mill and up the slope by a flight of old stone steps. There are some good houses to be seen along the quarter-mile climb to the church. Just past Top Farm there is a stile set into the wall on your right. Cross the stile and head directly towards the church: there you can enter the churchyard by a massive stone stile set into the perimeter wall as you approach it.

Tellisford church was much restored by the Victorians, but it must not be dismissed as unworthy of a visit. It is diminutive in size, consisting only of tower, nave and chancel and possesses a simplicity which is immediately appealing. There is a Norman arch with zigzag pattern over the door and some interesting fragments of sculpture inside which originated from the old village cross which was situated near the church from the fourteenth century. These fragments were discovered in the fabric of the church during nineteenth-century restoration work.

Leave the church by the path leading from the porch. Bear left at the junction and follow the lane for almost a mile down to Rode Bridge.

The ruined mill buildings here represent yet another old woollen mill, although latterly used as a corn mill.

Tellisford Bridge, looking across the River Frome from Somerset to Wiltshire

Bear left and cross the bridge, past a handsome Georgian house and a group of buildings which include stables and a summer house with a Venetian window. Rode and the village green is reached by taking the next turning on the right.

Alternative short walk from Rode to Tellisford along the River Frome:

Leave the village green and head through the village towards its southern edge. Just past an abandoned ornamental garden on your right, bear right along a street with local authority houses on your right. Pretty soon the tarmac ends and the road reverts to a narrow track that leads gently downhill. You reach a point where there are stiles on either side; bear right across the stile and into a riverside meadow. The right of way heads diagonally across the field towards a point just to the right of a group of derelict farm buildings. From here make for the gate above which leads you to the main road. Bear right and then left by a track past Langham House on your left and Christ Church on your right.

Christ Church was built in 1824; Pevsner describes the exterior as 'amazing' and it certainly is very different.

The track gradually descends to the valley bottom. Do not take the right fork to Langham Farm but stay on the lower path, past a weir which controlled the stream to the former Langham Mill and on towards the house on the river bank. Pass the house and outbuildings on your left and go through a gate to reach a field. Now follow the river, which here marks the Somerset–Wiltshire border, cross a stile, walk past another weir and on to Tellisford Bridge.

14 SOUTH WRAXALL

via Monkton Farleigh, Farleigh Wick, Little Ashley and Great Cumberwell

Distance: 7 ½ miles

THE WALK, though a good distance, does not entail any steep slopes. Most of the route is by field paths and green tracks, with a shorter section along lanes which carry little traffic. South Wraxall and Monkton Farleigh are both attractive and interesting villages; there are pubs in both and at Farleigh Wick, which is nearer to halfway along the route.

To begin the walk, make for the centre of South Wraxall, in the vicinity of the pub and church.

South Wraxall is a scattered village: the distance between the Manor House and Farm to the north and Home Farm to the south is about a mile on foot and rather farther by road. There are, in fact, three distinct nuclei to the village: the Manor House and Farm form a northerly group, the church and pub a centre group, whilst Lower Wraxall comprises a number of farms, houses and cottages.

St James Church is most notable for its tower with prominent stair turret and saddle-back roof. The tower dates from *c*. 1300; Pevsner describes it as 'picturesque', but I find that the introduction of oblique angles into a structure whose lines should be essentially vertical lends a jarring note. Inside, the church contains the Long Chapel, where generations of lords of the Manor of South Wraxall lie interred. Close by the church is the former school, dated 1841, and now the village hall.

Take the lane opposite the Long Arms pub beside the church. The lane eventually bears right: just after this bend look out for a turning on the left and follow the track round towards the short terrace of cottages ahead. Cross two wooden stiles just to the left of these cottages and then follow the field boundary on the left to a stile in the top left corner of the field — here you enter the lane outside South Wraxall Manor House.

Pevsner says of South Wraxall Manor that 'the house is an outstandingly successful mixture of the fifteenth century and the later Elizabethan and Jacobean. Moreover, what features of both periods remain are outstanding

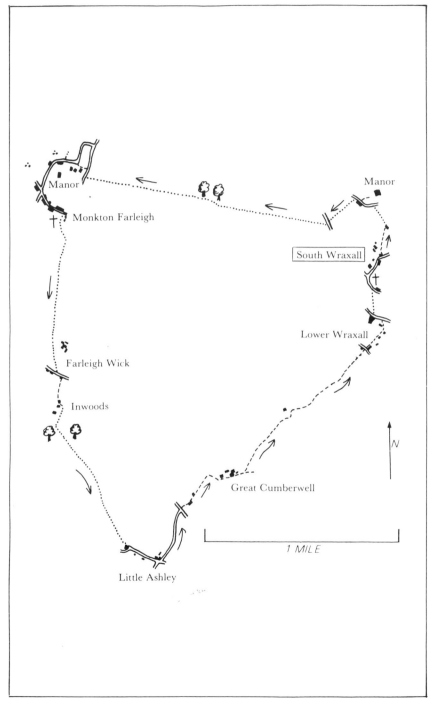

Manor

Manor

Monkton Farleigh

South Wraxall

Farleigh Wick

Lower Wraxall

Inwoods

Great Cumberwell

N

1 MILE

Little Ashley

in their own right.' However, the house is privately owned and is not open to the public. The little that can be seen is certainly enticing: the gate house with immaculate oriel window over the archway, the enormous drawing-room window on the west front, which was added to the north of the hall in the late sixteenth century and, in the garden facing the road, the domed, octagonal summer house. South Wraxall Manor was the home of the Longs from the early fifteenth century until quite recently in the present century. It is said that the first tobacco smoked in England was smoked here in the Manor House.

Beyond the Manor to the east is the Manor Farm, the farmhouse of which was originally a hospice for poor travellers and dates from the fourteenth century. Little or nothing of this is visible from the road, however.

Bear left along the lane for a quarter mile and go through two gates to the left immediately after a farmhouse. Go straight across the field to the stile on the opposite boundary. Climb this and cross the next field to join the road opposite. The pair of iron gates and gateposts here originally formed part of the grand drive between Monkton Farleigh and South Wraxall Manors. Cross the wooden stile just beyond the far gatepost and proceed to walk the 1⅓ miles straight ahead to the lane below Monkton Farleigh Manor, whose Georgian façade is clearly visible on elevated ground in the distance. You cross a couple of stiles on the way to reach a stile beside a cottage below the big house.

The most direct route from here to the church and the village main street is to turn left and then right. However, there are objects of interest to be seen by making a circular tour of the village. To do so, bear right on reaching the lane below the Manor House, then left, not up the first opening which simply leads to a farm, but by the lane beyond. The lane bears left, then right, until you reach the north gate to the Manor.

Opposite this is a public footpath sign indicating a right of way to Kingsdown. If you cross the stile here into the field you can find a large area scooped out of the slope which is all that now remains of the fish ponds used by the monks of the Cluniac priory of Monkton Farleigh, founded in 1125, and sited where the Manor House now stands. Little evidence remains of the priory, save for a few stone fragments, a pair of lancet windows and some thirteenth-century stone effigies. None of this is visible from the road.

Beyond the northern gateway the lane bears left.

Once past the cottages on the right, you can see, at the far side of the field to your right, a small, solitary building with a steep pitched roof. This is the ancient Monks Conduit, where a spring of water was utilised to supply the priory and still does supply several houses in the village.

Bear left at the road ahead, opposite the Kings Arms pub.

This is the village main street, with the stone cottages falling away to St Peter's Church which, apart from its thirteenth-century tower, was largely

St James Church, South Wraxall

rebuilt by the Victorians. One unusual feature is the holy-water stoop set into the wall at the entrance gate.

Immediately beyond the church, take the signposted public footpath to Farleigh Wick. Beyond the churchyard you cross a stile into a field, then follow the barbed-wire fence on the right towards a kissing gate in the hedgerow. Cross into the next field and make for a stile near the bottom corner, then follow the hedgebank on the left. At the top left corner cross into a further field and follow the hedgebank on the right. Cross the stone wall at the top and head across the next field towards a wooden stile, then towards a stile in the bottom left corner of the next field. There remains one last field to cross: head diagonally across this field just to the left of the wind pump and towards the stile at the bottom left corner. You now drop down on to the main road near the Fox and Hounds pub.

To continue the walk, bear left towards the gateway with stone pillars at the end of the conglomeration of buildings which comprise Farleigh Wick. Enter the gateway and walk up the drive towards 'Inwoods'. Where the drive forks, bear left towards the group of buildings ahead. Pass through the gate on the left and into a field. Turn right and follow the boundary wall of Inwoods. Bear left at the top right-hand corner of this field towards the gate below. Once through the gate you keep to the left and head down towards the barbed-wire fence where the crossing point is marked by some old plastic fertiliser bags wrapped around the barbed wire.

The next section of the walk is not so easy to navigate. You need to continue in the same south-westerly direction: as you head across the field you reach a hump where you will be able to see a cluster of buildings on the hill top ahead and a gate by which you enter the field ahead. Once in the field you can follow the hedgebank on the right which will lead you to those buildings and then to the lane to Little Ashley. Bear left at the staggered crossroads at Little Ashley and follow the lane down towards the main road. Cross the road and take the track opposite towards Great Cumberwell Farm. The track swings right under a stone wall and then left past the farmhouse and outbuildings. Once past Great Cumberwell the track forks: bear left under a row of large horse-chestnuts and straight on towards Cherry Tree Farm, where the track becomes a lane and leads directly to South Wraxall. At Lower Wraxall cross the lane and carry straight on by another lane, then through a kissing gate into a field. Follow the path to another kissing gate and bear left by the sixteenth-century Mison's Farm. Cross the road to another well-marked path and through three kissing gates to Church Fields and the pub and church at the centre of the village.

15 SOUTHSTOKE

via Tucking Mill, Midford and the Somerset Coal Canal

Distance: 4 miles

THE WALK provides a good half day's ramble but with a sharp ascent back to the village. A derelict canal and railways give this walk added interest. There are pubs at Southstoke and Midford.

Southstoke is an attractive village set in a hollow between Odd Down and Hodshill, its buildings well grouped around the crossroads and small sloping green at its centre. St James Church has a low perpendicular tower; its main feature of interest is its intricately carved Norman doorway. The carvings have rather too crisp edges, probably indicating the work done during the restoration of 1845 — indeed, the entire right-hand pillar was replaced at that time. Sketches on display inside show the church after the 1712 rebuilding and before and after the 1845 restoration. Beyond the church is Manor Farm and barn. The barn dates from *c.* 1500 and includes a dovecote, still used as such, beyond the central porch.

To begin the walk, leave the village by the lane at the top of the green which leads away from the village in the opposite direction to the church. After about a quarter of a mile look for a gap in the hedge on the left where a signposted public footpath leads over a stile and across a field to a gate in the far right corner. Cross the main road and make for the signpost and stile on the opposite side. Cross the stile and follow the hedgerow on the left.

As you progress downhill towards Horsecombe Vale you cross three stiles and at the fourth you cross into a field on the left. Ahead is a fifth stile and, beyond that, in the valley bottom, a footbridge (a couple of railway sleepers) across a stream. Now you enter a wood by a stile. Notice the boundary stone on your left, dated 1894 and marking the boundary between the City of Bath and Somerset. Follow the path along the valley, slightly above the stream, first through a wood, then across a field, then again through woods. You emerge from this last section of wood to find a group of buildings before you. These form part of the Wessex Water Authority's complex at Tucking Mill.

Continue by passing through a kissing gate and hiking up the valley on your left. Notice the cutting of the former Somerset and Dorset branch railway to the right as it prepares to enter the tunnel under Combe Down. Bear right above the tunnel entrance, through a pair of kissing gates, and descend by a footpath on the east side of the cutting. The cutting soon becomes an embankment before the line finally crosses Horsecombe Vale

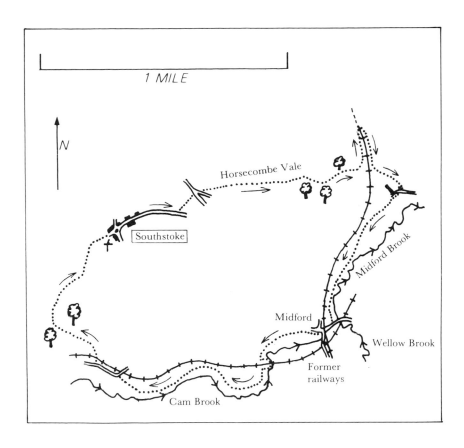

1 MILE

N

Horsecombe Vale

Southstoke

Midford Brook

Midford

Wellow Brook

Former
railways

Cam Brook

by a viaduct. The footpath enters woods and diverges to the left above Tucking Mill reservoir. You continue to descend, past a house and then on to a lane. Here you bear right.

Notice the house on the right with its tablet commemorating the fact that William Smith lived here when he was employed as engineer on the Somerset Coal Canal. William Smith is known as the 'Father of English Geology' because he it was who established the orderly succession of strata in the earth's crust and that each layer can be identified by the fossil remains it contains. Smith went on to conduct a geological survey of the country around Bath and drew some of the first geological maps. These may be seen in the geological collection at Bath Reference Library where there is a permanent exhibit on William Smith.

Cross the lane and the wooded fence on the far side. You now follow the footpath inside the fence all the way to Midford.

Bridge over disused Somerset Coal Canal, near Midford

This footpath follows the course of the old Somerset Coal Canal. This is not immediately obvious but after a few hundred yards the familiar cross section of a canal situated in a river valley becomes clear. To your left is a man-made embankment which drops away to the riverside meadow. To your right is the shallow basin of the canal whilst you are walking along the old towpath. The Midford Brook from Midford itself down to the Avon marks the former boundary of Somerset and Wiltshire, so that Limpley Stoke and the hill behind it are a part of Wiltshire.

On reaching the main road at Midford bear right. The next stage of the route is indicated by a signpost opposite the Hope and Anchor pub.

The two disused railway viaducts at Midford are like a couple of stranded dinosaurs of the railway age. The larger one beside the pub carried the Somerset and Dorset line from Bath, whilst the smaller, which no longer spans the road, carried the Cam Valley line from Limpley Stoke.

Follow the footpath under the viaduct. Cross a wooden stile and a few yards to the left you will find the raised towpath of the canal.

Along the first few yards of the towpath you may notice the exposed rockface on the opposite bank. These strata are the Midford Sands, a friable sandstone which is a local variation in the Liassic formation. The bridge over the Cam Brook on the left marks the course of an aborted branch of the Somerset Coal Canal: this was as far as it got. Farther along, just before the railway embankment which is built across the canal and completely blocks it off, there is another stone bridge looking slightly ridiculous as it spans a dried-out and grassed-over canal bed in a cow field.

Now you must cross the railway by passing under the bridged section over the Cam Brook. Cross the stile ahead and bear left towards the stream, then right along the water's edge and under the railway bridge. Bear right past the bridge, then left over a wooden stile to continue the walk along the towpath.

This section through unspoilt country is the most rewarding of the walk. After wet weather the canal is full of water and really looks like a canal. One of the few reminders of the twentieth century is the Combe Hay municipal rubbish dump in the distance ahead. Here use is being made of the former cutting of the old Camerton branch line, under which you have just passed.

Farther along you encounter a series of three locks, the stonework still pretty much intact. After the third lock the towpath reaches a wooden stile. Cross the stile and turn right up a path to the lane above. Bear left here towards Combe Hay. Opposite Bridge Farm Piggeries you bear right under a brick railway arch and follow the canal towpath once again. The path is found on the right, keeping the basin on your left. You will pass by a further five locks before the canal takes a hairpin bend to the left through the woods.

85

This wood is named on the 2½" O.S. map as 'Engine Wood' and it was here that the former caisson lock was constructed which raised barges 46 feet up the hillside. The caisson was a failure and was replaced by an inclined plane and finally by a flight of locks. Further disused locks and the fallen masonry of the engine house may be found in Engine Wood.

To return to Southstoke cross the stile ahead and follow the path keeping the stream on your left. The path bears right to ascend the hill, passing to the left of a derelict house, then by a track by the edge of a wood. Climb the field ahead and head for an iron stile in the edge of the field at the top right. This drops you into a lane which leads directly to Southstoke, the barn, the church and the green in the village centre.

OLD LOCK ON THE SOMERSET COAL CANAL

16   ST CATHERINE'S

via St Catherine's Valley

Distance: 3½ miles

THE WALK is along the delectable valley of St Catherine's. There is a field path which runs beside the brook; there is also a quiet lane higher up the hillside and a number of points where the brook may be crossed. Thus it is possible to visit St Catherine's Church (which alone is open to the public), see the Court and tithe barn, and then embark on a ramble along the brook in either direction and to return by the lane. The route described here is a narrow loop from St Catherine's Court upstream as far as a point below The Grey House where the brook is crossed by stepping stones before ascending to the lane for the return. Back at St Catherine's the walk continues by the lane to return by the field path just upstream from The Mead Tea Gardens. The walk is therefore as short or as long as you wish to make it.

Parking on the lane in St Catherine's Valley can be a problem. The lane widens near the Court and it is advisable to park under the trees before the Court gates are reached.

St Catherine's was originally a possession of Bath Abbey, the Court and church being built in the late 1400s. According to a leaflet written and kindly supplied by the present owner, the building dates from the fifteenth century, with the exception of the library wing and the orangery, which were added in 1919 but built in the original Tudor style.

St Catherine's Church contains a representation of Prior Cantlow in the fine stained glass dated 1490. There is an impressive monument to William Blanchard (died 1631), and his wife, in the form of two life-size kneeling figures on the north side of the chancel. The whole group at St Catherine's: the Court, the church and the tithe barn make a most beautiful ensemble, the weathered stone of these attractive old buildings set against the green, wooded hillside. The best view is perhaps from the footpath below, approaching from the south, a point included in the route of the walk.

To begin the walk, make for the kissing gate opposite the entrance to St Catherine's Court. Once you have entered the field, head diagonally across and down to the left-hand corner towards a wooden stile. Continue downhill to another stile beside St Catherine's

Brook, then on to a footbridge across the brook. Once across the footbridge you simply follow the field path with the brook on your left.

You eventually reach the ruins of an old stone building. Make your way around the back of this building (the right-hand side as you approach it). You now reach a track leading into a field which rises up to Ayford Farm. Climb this short incline to a point somewhat to the left of the farm building: here you will find a stile by which you leave the field and enter a lane. Bear left down towards the bridge across the brook.

Just before you reach the bridge you cross a double wooden stile on your right in order to continue the walk along the brookside path. Simply keep to the brook to pass through a succession of fields. You have to negotiate in order: a stile, a gate, then four more stiles. After the last stile, head down towards the brook. In a bend of the brook shaded by tall trees, there are stepping stones leading to a wooden stile on the opposite bank.

Once across the stile and into a sloping field, make your way directly up this rather steep incline towards a stile at the top, just to the right of The Grey House. This drops you down into a lane where you bear left and make your way back to St Catherine's Court.

Before you leave the stile and make your way back along the lane it is worth pausing to take in the view. There is a panorama of hills and vales towards the west, north and east. Marshfield is on the summit of the hill to the north and you begin to feel that here you are truly in the foothills of the Cotswolds. The lane itself is at a higher level than the brookside path and affords a complimentary view of the valley.

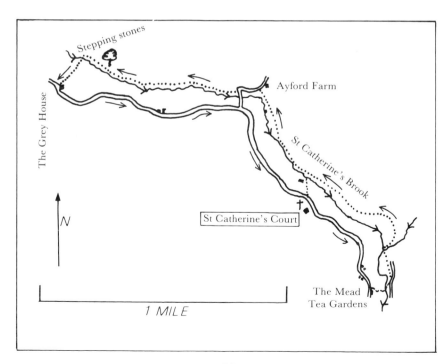

St Catherine's Church seen through the gateposts to the Court

From St Catherine's Court continue along the lane towards Batheaston. After just over half a mile, look out for a signpost marking the course of a bridleway, beside a house on the left (The Mead Tea Gardens is the next house down the lane). Follow this path down to a footbridge across the brook and bear left at the lane. Now enter the field ahead on the left where a yellow arrow indicates the right of way. The course of the footpath all the way back towards St Catherine's Court is now given by a series of yellow arrows which makes the going quite clear.

As you cross the last stile below St Catherine's you will observe a pair of yellow arrows pointing in each direction beside the brook. Just to the left is the footbridge across the brook which leads to the field path up the hillside towards the kissing gate on the lane opposite the Court.

17 STEEPLE ASHTON

via Ashton Hill and Rood Ashton

Distance: 4 miles

THE WALK is an easy half day's ramble with no steep climbs. It passes through open, agricultural country and affords some good views towards Salisbury Plain. There is a pub in Steeple Ashton.

Steeple Ashton is one of Wiltshire's most attractive villages and one of its best conserved, as the plaques opposite the village green which record several successes in the Best Kept Village competition testify.

The church is unavoidable: its multitudinous pinnacles leap up like so many exclamation marks and compel the walker to look long and admiringly. St Mary's is a large and magnificent church and a reminder of the great prosperity which the wool and cloth trade brought to this community in the past. Inside the church there is stone vaulting in all parts but the nave, which has a wooden roof. The steeple, which formerly reached a height of 186 feet, collapsed in 1670.

In addition to the church, this sizeable village exhibits a collection of houses distinctive in the variety of periods, styles and materials employed in their building. There are houses built of stone, but also of brick; there are some of both materials. There are one or two stone roofs, but more of tile or slate or thatch. There are cruck-built cottages, timber-framed houses and scaled-down Georgian town houses. There is a village green with a blind house and a village cross, dated 1679, with a sundial.

Leave the churchyard by the metal gate to the west of the tower and follow the tarmac path as far as the stile on the right. Climb this and turn left to cross the field diagonally to a stile near the far corner. Cross this stile and follow the left edge of the field to the far corner where you cross another stile and drop down into the road. Follow the road out of the village for about half a mile towards a group of cottages comprising the hamlet of Ashton Hill which takes its name from the eminence to its south west.

About 100 yards beyond the end of the pavement and almost opposite 'Rose Cottage', look for a track which leads away from the main road to the left. This track is indicated on the 2½" O.S. map as Mudmead Lane and it certainly lives up to its name in wet weather, especially in its lower reaches. The track climbs gently and eventually becomes a wide green lane, running between fields bordered by trees. Mudmead Lane runs for about a mile and reaches its highest point, around 270 feet, about halfway along its course. It provides an exhilarating route through unspoilt country and added interest is provided by the wide variety of wild flowers which grow here, encouraged by the diversity of strata underlying Ashton Hill.

Here there are good views to the west over Trowbridge and the clay vale. On the summit of the hill, on your left, is a disused quarry working, marked by a line of trees on its crest. Limestone was dug here. Lower down the lane, the soil underfoot will be found on examination to contain much sand and grit. Ashton Hill, like Steeple Ashton and the surrounding country, lies on the Corallian beds which comprise layers of sand, clay and limestone. Mudmead Lane descends to a junction with Sandpits Lane leading off to the left back towards Steeple Ashton.

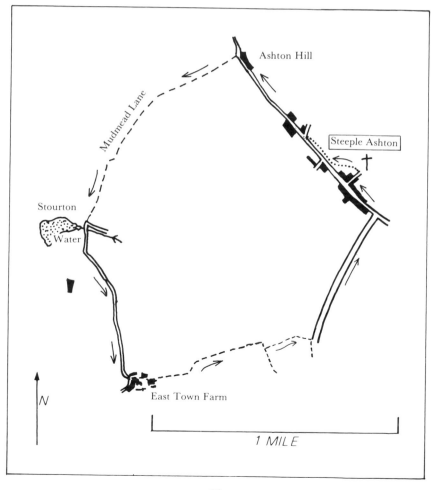

The village green, Steeple Ashton.

93

At the foot of Mudmead Lane there is a public footpath on the right leading past Stourton Water and through fields towards Trowbridge. However, you carry straight on along the quiet lane ahead. Home Farm is on your right, with a walled garden beyond, and behind them what remains of the wooded park of Rood Ashton. Continue climbing towards the small settlement beyond. Here you bear left through East Town Farm, away from the metalled road, past a row of cottages on your left, and an assortment of farm buildings on your right and, farther along on your left, a windpump. Follow this track and gently descend.

This is wide open agricultural country and there are wonderful views towards the downs and, nearer at hand, that compelling vista of Steeple Ashton church. This somewhat elevated country has something of the feel of the chalk downs.

After a dog leg junction you ascend to reach a T-junction: here bear left along the track which leads directly to the village, past the pub, village green and back to the church.

'I turned out of my way to see Steeple Ashton. It has no steeple, being in fact Staple Ashton, but a tower and a dial on a church, a very big church, bristling with coarse crockets all over, and knobby with coarse gargoyles, half lion and half dog, some spewing down, some out, some up. It is not a show village, like Lacock, where the houses are packed as in a town, and most of the gardens invisible; but a happy alternation of cottages of stone or brick (sometimes placed herring-bone fashion) or timber work, vegetable gardens, orchard plots, and the wagon maker's. On many a wagon for miles round the name of Steeple Ashton is painted. It is on level ground, but well up towards the plain, over the wall of which rounded clouds, pure white and sunlit, were heaving up . . .'

Edward THOMAS, *In Pursuit of Spring*, Thomas Nelson, 1914.

18 UPTON SCUDAMORE

via Norridge, Chapmanslade and Thoulstone

Distance: 6½ miles

THE WALK is a relatively long one along old tracks and field paths, with a little road walking. There are long stretches along what appear to be remote tracks far from human habitation. If you enjoy a more challenging walk then you might enjoy this route with its sunken, overgrown tracks and large open fields and the feeling of isolation from the human world. There are pubs at Upton Scudamore and Chapmanslade.

Upton Scudamore is so named because it is situated some four hundred feet up on a spur of lower chalk which juts out to the west from Salisbury Plain; the Scudamores were lords of the manor since Norman times. The village church of St Mary was largely rebuilt by the Victorians, and the plain tower a century before, although it does retain a good Norman arch. There are few buildings of antiquity in this rather workaday village although the Manor Farmhouse is partly medieval.

With your back to Upton Scudamore church, bear left along the lane, past Millards Farm and on towards the edge of the village where the land slopes gently down to the west. At a point where the road bears sharply towards the right, make for the gate straight ahead. Once through the gate continue in the same direction towards a bridge which crosses the railway, then continue in a straight line across fields and by hedgebanks until you reach a disused stretch of road. This used to be part of the A36 Bath–Warminster road but has been replaced by a new stretch a little farther to the west.

Bear left and cross a stile just before the old road joins the new. Now cross the road and continue by the grass verge a short distance to the entrance to Norridge Farm. Bear right and pass farm buildings on the left, then left through a gate just after the entrance drive to a grand new house. Pass through a second gate ahead to enter a field. Now head diagonally across this field to the near right-hand corner. Here there is a gate which leads into a long narrow field at the far end of which is another gate. The path now follows the edge of a wood for about half a mile. At the end of a wood is a gate leading into a field.

From here you can see the long line of buildings of Chapmanslade standing prominently on the ridge about a mile to the north west.

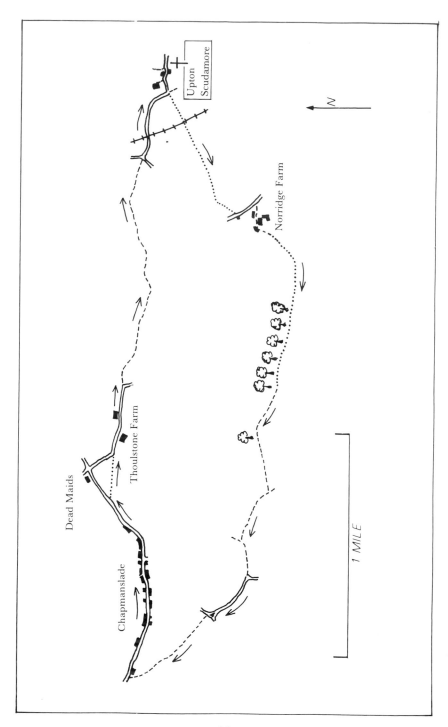

Upton Scudamore

Norridge Farm

Thoulstone Farm

Dead Maids

Chapmanslade

N

1 MILE

Follow the hedgebank on the left to the bottom left corner and pass through another gate. From here the right of way is a fairly wide track with a hedgebank on either side. You eventually reach a T-junction where you bear right. The track now becomes more sunken as it heads downhill. The proximity of a lane is heralded by mounds of hardcore and other rubbish which have been dumped along the course of the track here. At the end of the track carry on to reach the lane which runs between Corsley and Chapmanslade. At the minor junction ahead, at the point where a second lane joins the main one as it begins to rise towards Chapmanslade, look out for a signposted public bridleway which continues in the same direction you have been following. This is one of those old, sunken roads and carries you uphill for about half a mile until you reach the main road towards the western edge of Chapmanslade and almost within shouting distance of the Wiltshire–Somerset border (Frome is about three miles to the west).

There are some good exposures of Upper Greensand along the sides of the track: Chapmanslade itself is built on a ridge formed by an outcrop of this rock. The place name Chapmanslade literally means 'the road of the chapmen', or pedlars, and one can imagine that long road crossing the county boundary and linking Westbury and Frome being a favourite meeting place of chapmen.

Bear right at the main road and walk through Chapmanslade, a somewhat uneventful village. There is a shop and a pub, 'The Three Horseshoes', in the centre. Beyond the eastern edge of the village, look out for a stile on the right-hand side of the road, under a road sign. Enter the field here and head towards a stile on the opposite edge of the field, just before the group of buildings at Thoulstone Farm.

The house at the junction to the left is known by the unusual name of Dead Maids. The origin of this name lies in a rather gruesome story which begins in Black Dog Wood, a little to the north. A local farmer's daughter had two suitors, each unknown to the other, one of whom owned a black dog. When they discovered each other's intentions the two men fought until the owner of the dog was killed. At this the dog killed his master's slayer and the farmer's daughter committed suicide and was buried at Dead Maids Cross.*

This further stile drops you down into the road which leads past Thoulstone Farm.

An interesting feature at Thoulstone is to be seen on the left of the drive just beyond the farmhouse. There is here an old granary still intact: a wooden structure standing upon staddle stones. Staddle stones, of course, are a favourite piece of garden furniture and one can see them in many pub and private gardens in the countryside. But here they are still in their original position: supporting a wooden granary and protecting grain, once stored here, from attack by vermin.

*This story is quoted in the following:
Kathleen WILTSHIRE, *Ghosts and Legends of the Wiltshire Countryside*, Compton Russell, 1973.

Old granary, Thoulstone Farm, near Chapmanslade

Cross over the main road ahead and make for the section of disused road to the right of the buildings. Do not follow the disused road as it bears right to rejoin the new road, but carry on towards the grassy track ahead. The track makes its way between hedgebanks for over half a mile until a stile is reached which drops you down on to a lane. Continue by the lane opposite, which crosses the railway to reach Millards Farm and Upton Scudamore church.

GREEN LANE

19 WELLOW

via Baggridge Hill and Stoney Littleton

Distance: 6 miles

THE WALK is a pleasing and varied one. The route leaves Wellow to follow the Wellow Brook down stream, then heads up a tributary valley towards Norton St Philip, branching off to climb Baggridge Hill and reach a point above five hundred feet. From here the descent is through a wood, then by bridleway and field path, via Stoney Littleton Long Barrow, and back to Wellow. It is advisable to take a torch on this ramble if you wish to explore the inner recesses of Stoney Littleton Long Barrow, and it is quite safe to do so. There is a pub in Wellow.

Wellow is a spacious and attractive village and an essentially linear one which stretches for over half a mile along a road which is paralleled by the course of the former Cam Valley branch railway. The village is situated on a south-facing slope at between two and three hundred feet, and there are a few more cottages beside the lane which leads down to the ford and footbridge across Wellow Brook.

The pride of Wellow is its very handsome church, which stands in a commanding position at the northern edge of the village. The church dates back to 1372, which is a comparatively late date for the origin of the village churches visited on these rambles. Wellow, in fact, is one of the very few villages in the area which is not mentioned in the Domesday Book.

St Julian's Church is particularly attractive inside because of the architectural consistency it displays — this in place of the jumble of periods and styles to which one is accustomed in village churches. The chancel was, in fact, rebuilt in 1890 but is a sympathetic restoration. The clerestory windows throw ample light on the proud and uncluttered interior. The intricate carving of the rood screen and the colourful sculptures in the Hungerford chapel provide a striking counterpoint to the bare grey stone of the main structure. This really is an outstanding church and time is required to savour its delights. St Julian's Well springs up in a little valley north east of the church: there is a footpath to this point but there is nothing much to see, save a charming, secluded glen.

Wellow bridge and ford

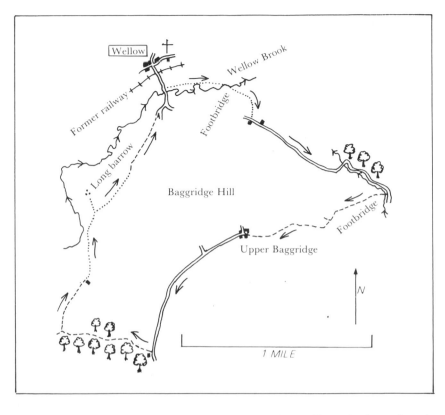

To begin the walk, take the lane leading down beside the village school past the twin piers of the former railway bridge, and down towards Wellow Brook. The bridge is only for pedestrians; vehicular traffic must use the ford which is generally above the level of the brook but which is quite submerged by a rushing torrent after rain. Just before the ford, look out for a stile on the left: cross over here to enter a field. Wellow Brook meanders its way down the valley to the right — simply follow the general eastward course of the brook without sticking to its every twist and turn.

As you enter a second field, however, you should stick fairly closely to the river bank after about two hundred yards in order to locate a footbridge across the brook. Once on the opposite bank the right of way crosses the field diagonally to reach the row of trees on the hillside. Follow the trees on the right to enter a field on the right; then follow the hedgebank on the right uphill to the lane opposite Wellow Farm. Bear left and follow the lane now for about a mile, past Norton Lane Farm, down and over a bridge which crosses a tributary of the Wellow Brook, then through woods.

Look out for a layby on the right: here there is a path leading to the stream. From here follow a well-worn path beside the stream to a ford and footbridge and the next stage of the walk. At the footbridge, take the track which leads uphill. You first reach a junction where the right fork leads to Lower Baggridge. Keep straight on at this point, through the gate ahead. You now follow the track to a second gate and then follow a stone wall on your right as you approach the summit of the hill and Upper Baggridge Farm.

102

Looking out from Stoney Littleton long barrow

From this high and windy ridge there is a fine view in all directions: east and south towards Salisbury Plain, Cley Hill and the woods of Longleat, across to Wellow and a mile to the west of the village centre, on the sloping hillside and just below a small copse, the scar left by a vanished Roman villa. Up the valley to the west it is possible to see the pyramidal spoil heaps, now quite overgrown, and some villages associated with the now abandoned Somerset Coalfield.

From Upper Baggridge, follow the ridge-top road for almost a mile in a south-westerly direction, until you reach a house on the edge of a wood. Here bear right along a wide track which descends the wooded hillside. This is a pretty half mile's walk which brings you out on to a lane where you bear right by a track between fields. At the building ahead enter a field and make for a stile in the far top left corner. To do this it is necessary to descend and ascend the hillside.

Once across this stile and into the next field, the right of way follows the hedgebank on the right, but you will no doubt want to see at close quarters, the long barrow which rises up out of the hillside like a great beached whale. A path leads to the fenced enclosure and the gate which gives access to the barrow.

Stoney Littleton Long Barrow dates from the Bronze Age of four thousand years ago. It is an excellent example of a Cotswold-type long barrow which was used to inter members of the same family or clan over many generations. The door jambs (one of which displays a splendid ammonite cast) support a huge lintel and lead to three pairs of burial chambers on either side of a central gallery. It is quite possible to penetrate the farthest recesses of the ancient tomb, some 50 feet from the entrance, and to inspect the fine stonework of its construction. It is strangely moving to enter this barrow and to be conscious that men were burying their dead on this Somerset hillside two thousand years before Christ.

From the long barrow, make your way back to the stile and continue by following the hedgebank on the right, then cross a field in which the hedge has been removed, towards the entrance to a track between hedgebanks which leads down to a lane and the footbridge and ford over Wellow Brook.

20 WESTWOOD

via Stowford, Farleigh Castle and Iford

Distance: 3½ miles

THE WALK: Although an easy, short walk the route includes two manor houses, an outstanding parish church, a fifteenth-century mill and a fourteenth-century castle, as well as a beautiful stretch of the River Frome. This walk does include a few hundred yards of road walking. There is a pub at Farleigh Hungerford, though not directly on the route of this walk.

Westwood Manor and church make a splendid group of ancient buildings on the edge of the village. The Manor belongs to the National Trust and is open to the public on Wednesdays in the summer months. The church is normally kept locked except on these Wednesdays. It is difficult to do the Manor and church justice in a few lines, particularly as there are excellent guide books available on both.

Westwood Manor is a diminutive building, in comparison with Great Chalfield or South Wraxall, and has portions dating from *c.* 1400, the late fifteenth century and 1610. It was the rich clothier Thomas Horton, who is commemorated in Holy Trinity Church in Bradford-on-Avon, who lived here and extended the house in the early 1600s. A fifteenth-century stone barn is sited to the east of the Manor whilst the church of St Mary is very close, being just to the south. The main feature of the church is its elaborate Somerset-type tower. The Manor, especially, will repay a visit, when you will enjoy a guided tour.

Opposite Westwood church there is a pair of public footpath signs, one pointing to Farleigh Hungerford and one to Stowford. Take the route to Stowford which leads directly across the field towards a clump of willows which surround a small pond. Make for the stile to the left of the pond and climb over into the next field. You can see Midway Manor away to the left and Salisbury Plain in the distance ahead. Continue straight on but soon bear a little to the right: head towards a hedgerow which you keep on your left. Continue to descend gently towards the group of old stone buildings in the valley bottom. As you approach the road you pass through a gate with cowsheds on the left, then through another gate and into the road.

Stowford Mill, according to Kenneth Rogers, was leased by one William Sewey, clothman, in 1458, from Keynsham Abbey, so it may have been used as a fulling mill from that date. Its most prosperous time was the fifteenth century when the present house was built. Stowford was used as a centre for the production of wool and cloth for four centuries; in the mid-nineteenth century it became a corn mill.

Bear right and follow the road to Farleigh Hungerford. The River Frome meanders through meadows just below the road but, unfortunately, there is no public footpath by the river bank, although there is a grass verge farther on where the road ascends and looks down on to a weir. As you approach Farleigh Hungerford the road bears left over a pair of bridges which cross the River Frome and the mill stream respectively.

The old mill stood on the island between the two waterways and was the last country mill to close down; a fulling mill was recorded here in 1548 which was worked till 1910. There is a row of houses on the right-hand bank, including a former chapel, dated 1850. Over all loom the ruined walls and towers of Farleigh Hungerford Castle.

Farleigh Castle is open to the public, being maintained by the Department of the Environment. A leaflet is obtainable, from which the following sketch is largely culled. The original castle dates from the 1370s and was built by Sir Thomas Hungerford, a Wiltshire squire who was Speaker of the House of Commons in 1377. He died in 1398 and is buried in an enormous tombchest in the chapel within the castle. His son, Sir Walter Hungerford, also a Speaker of the House of Commons, extended the castle by adding an outer court to enclose the former parish church and built the new church of St Leonard up the hill. Farleigh twice fell out of the possession of the Hungerfords and was twice repossessed. In the Civil War, the heir to Farleigh was commander of the Parliamentary forces in Wiltshire, and

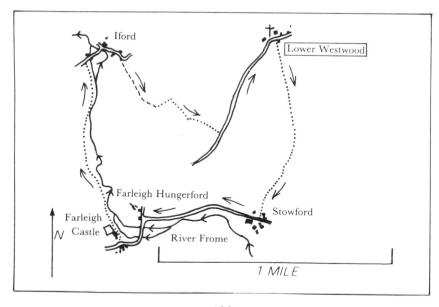

Farleigh Castle

defeated his Royalist half-brother who had formerly occupied the castle. A later Hungerford, known as 'The Spendthrift', sold Farleigh in 1686, and it passed through various hands until placed under the guardianship of the Ministry of Works in 1919.

From the castle, take the path which leads down towards the mill stream from the car park outside the main gate. Bear left at the track below and follow it under the castle's eastern walls as far as the remains of the north-east tower. Once beyond the castle walls, cross a bridge over a minor brook which meets the mill stream just below.

Leave the metalled track below the house called 'Farleigh Springs' and keep close to the stream on your right. Cross a footbridge over a ditch to reach a stile on the far side, then cross a second stile just ahead. Once across this stile you follow the river bank through several fields until you reach the lane at Iford.

There is another weir at Iford which once controlled the flow of a mill stream that powered the former Iford Mill. The iron sluice gates can be seen at the head of the mill stream.

At the lane bear right past the old mill and over the bridge to Iford Manor (for description see Walk 1).

From Iford Manor bear right up the hill. Take the signposted bridleway a little way up on the right. This track climbs gently above the valley of the River Frome. The bridleway meets a brook ahead and bears to the right. There is a public footpath indicated through a field to the left. The bridleway provides some good views down the Frome valley towards the Avon but can be very muddy.

To take the footpath: enter the field on the left by a stile and follow the hedgebank on the left. Bear right at the field boundary ahead, then left and right again. Look out for a path between hedgebanks on the left. This leads you to the lane which links Farleigh Hungerford and Westwood. Bear left for Westwood — the church is the first part of the village to be reached.

FURTHER READING

An exhaustive list of books which might contain some information on those parts of Somerset and Wiltshire dealt with in this book of walks would run into many pages. Of the numerous guide books and topographical books which do exist a large proportion are, of course, out of print. Those of the present century which are not too difficult to come by include the Highways and Byways series, published by Macmillan. These superior books were in print for many years in various editions. Both the Somerset and Wiltshire titles were written by Edward Hutton and illustrated by Nelly Erichsen. Of the series, I rate these two volumes highly.

Another useful series are the Little Guides, originally published by Methuen. Each volume is arranged as a county gazetteer and, to some extent, the Little Guides were a precursor of Nikolaus Pevsner's Buildings of England series. A well-known series of county gazetteers is The King's England, edited by Arthur Mee and published by Hodder and Stoughton. Whilst I find the style of these books a little off putting in its effusiveness, they are interesting in that they include something on even the smallest village, if only an appreciation of the local church.

Another well-known series of county gazetteers are the Shell Guides, published by Faber. They are individual in approach and make an entertaining and informative source of reference. More up to date and currently in print is the incomparable Buildings of England series, edited by Nikolaus Pevsner and published by Penguin. These books comprise a thorough and exhaustive description of buildings of architectural interest, each one arranged as a county gazetteer. Although only available in an expensive hardback edition, these books are a really worthwhile reference source to anyone with an interest in the buildings around him.

The books described above are as follows:

Edward HUTTON
(Illustrated by Nelly Erichsen)
Highways and Byways in Somerset, Macmillan, 1912
Highways and Byways in Wiltshire, Macmillan, 1917

G. W. and J. H. WADE
The Little Guides: Somerset, Methuen, 1907

Frank R. HEATH
The Little Guides: Wiltshire, Methuen, 1911

Arthur MEE
The King's England: Somerset, Hodder and Stoughton
The King's England: Wiltshire, Hodder and Stoughton

J. H. CHEETHAM and John PIPER
Shell Guide to Wiltshire, Faber
Peter QUENNELL
Shell Guide to Somerset, Faber

Nikolaus PEVSNER
Buildings of England: North Somerset and Bristol, Penguin Books, 1958
Buildings of England: Wiltshire, Second edition revised by Bridget Cherry,
Penguin Books, 1975

One of the most useful books I have referred to in the compilation of this book has been *Wiltshire and Somerset Woollen Mills* by Wiltshire County Archivist, Kenneth Rogers. The gazetteer encapsulates a wealth of research under the headings of all the old woollen mills in the area where Somerset meets Wiltshire. In addition, there is a very interesting preliminary section which gives an account of the industry over the centuries:

Kenneth ROGERS
Wiltshire and Somerset Woollen Mills, Pasold Research Fund Ltd., Edington, Wiltshire, 1976

In addition to the books described above, I have listed below a section of the more recent books, most of which are in print at the time of writing, which I have found helpful in the appreciation of the landscape and buildings seen in the course of the walks described in this book:

D. V. AGER *et al*
Geologists' Association Guides No 36: The Cotswold Hills, Geologists' Association, 1973

R. S. BARRON
The Geology of Wiltshire, Moonraker Press, 1976

J. H. BETTEY
The Landscape of Wessex, Moonraker Press, 1980
Rural Life in Wessex, 1500–1900, Moonraker Press, 1977

C. A. and R. A. BUCHANAN
Batsford Guide to the Industrial Archaeology of the British Isles: Central Southern England, Batsford, 1980

C. P. CHATWIN
British Regional Geology: The Hampshire Basin and Adjoining Areas, H.M.S.O., 3rd edn, 1960

Kenneth R. CLEW
The Kennet and Avon Canal, David and Charles, 2nd edn, 1973
The Somersetshire Coal Canal and Railways, David and Charles, 1970

M. C. CORFIELD
A Guide to the Industrial Archaeology of Wiltshire, Wiltshire County Council Library and Museum Service, 1978

R. W. DUNNING
A History of Somerset, Somerset County Library, 1978

James DYER
Southern England: An Archaeological Guide, Faber, 1973

Jacquetta HAWKES
A Guide to the Prehistoric and Roman Monuments in England and Wales, Abacus, rev edn, 1973

Kenneth G. PONTING
Wool and Water: Bradford-on-Avon and the River Frome, Moonraker Press, 1975

David ST JOHN THOMAS
West Country Railway History, David and Charles, 5th rev edn, 1981

F. B. A. WELCH *et al*
British Regional Geology: Bristol and Gloucester District, H.M.S.O., 2nd edn, 1948

More books by Roger Jones from Ex Libris Press:

THE WALKER'S COMPANION

A Collection for all who enjoy the countryside on foot

The works of some 23 writers, beginning with Wordsworth and ending with Henry Williamson are quoted here and all illustrate some aspect of the walker's art. The urge to get away from it all and get close to nature opens us to the varied pleasures of walking: the pursuit of health, relaxation and renewal. All these are celebrated in prose and poetry. So too are the delights of the country footpath and mountain track, whether they be the fruits of a day's ramble or of an extended walking tour.

This remarkable collection of prose and verse . . . . a charming ramble of a book
Wiltshire Gazette and Herald

Illustrated with pen and ink sketches by Edward Dowden
A5 Paperback   112 pages   Price £2.95

Down the BRISTOL AVON
Including 14 Country Walks

The Bristol Avon springs to life in the foothills of the Gloucestershire Cotswolds. For much of its 75 miles it flows through the quiet and peaceful countryside of North and West Wiltshire by many of its pleasant and interesting towns and villages. Included among these are the hilltop town of Malmesbury, the outstanding National Trust village of Lacock and Bradford-on-Avon, 'the most beautiful little town in all Wiltshire'. The Avon rolls on through the incomparable Georgian city of Bath and the once great port of Bristol. Some of the more fascinating places and personalities associated with the Avon valley are recounted. In addition, some fourteen circular walks are described by which the reader may explore, at first hand, the countryside of the Bristol Avon.

It is well-researched and well-informed both as walker's guide and historical survey
Exploring Local History

Illustrated throughout with photographs, engravings and sketch maps
Uniform with *Where Wiltshire meets Somerset*   136 pages   Price £3.50

Available from bookshops or post free from the publishers:
Ex Libris Press, 1 The Shambles, Bradford-on-Avon, Wiltshire